MW00325420

THE SHAPE *of* MY HEART

THE SHAPE *of* MY HEART

A Pilgrimage Remembrance

RICHARD RAY

RESOURCE *Publications* · Eugene, Oregon

THE SHAPE OF MY HEART
A Pilgrimage Remembrance

Copyright © 2022 Richard Ray. All rights reserved. Except for brief quotations in critical publications or reviews, no part of this book may be reproduced in any manner without prior written permission from the publisher. Write: Permissions, Wipf and Stock Publishers, 199 W. 8th Ave., Suite 3, Eugene, OR 97401.

Resource Publications
An Imprint of Wipf and Stock Publishers
199 W. 8th Ave., Suite 3
Eugene, OR 97401

www.wipfandstock.com

PAPERBACK ISBN: 978-1-6667-3444-7
HARDCOVER ISBN: 978-1-6667-9029-0
EBOOK ISBN: 978-1-6667-9030-6

MARCH 21, 2022 12:45 PM

Unless otherwise noted, all photos are the author's.

All scripture from the *New American Bible, revised edition* © 2010, 1991, 1986, 1970 Confraternity of Christian Doctrine, Washington, D.C. and are used by permission of the copyright owner. All Rights Reserved. No part of the New American Bible may be reproduced in any form without permission in writing from the copyright owner.

This memoir is dedicated to Joe Strazanac, who was crazy to walk across an entire country, and crazier still to do it with me. God bless you, Joe.

My remembrances of the Camino de Santiago are also dedicated to my wife, Carol, who blessed my efforts to heal while she remained home suffering in her own way. She is my best friend.

For waters will burst forth in the wilderness,

and streams in the Arabah.

The burning sands will become pools,

and the thirsty ground, springs of water;

The abode where jackals crouch

will be a marsh for the reed and papyrus.

A highway will be there,

called the holy way;

No one unclean may pass over it,

but it will be for his people;

no traveler, not even fools, shall go astray on it.

No lion shall be there,

nor any beast of prey approach,

nor be found.

But there the redeemed shall walk,

And the ransomed of the Lord shall return,

and enter Zion singing,

crowned with everlasting joy;

They meet with joy and gladness,

sorrow and mourning flee away.

(Isa 35:6–10)

Contents

Preparing to Begin

T HERE's more than one kind of suffering.

I thought I'd toughened my feet up from the endless walking. I'd get home from an all-day hike of twenty miles or so, strip my socks off and stare at the natural disaster that was my feet. Flat where they should be gracefully arched. Pasty white, with crooked toes and blackened toenails. Callused in all the necessary places, or so I thought. Sometimes the skin on top of my feet was sprinkled with a million small, red bumps. Prickly heat. I thought I'd prepared my feet. Still, the long slog up the treadmill of stones that was the approach to the Matagrande Plain with its tantalizing view of Burgos on the far horizon reached through the soles of my Hoka trail runners and gave me my first blister. I felt the slightest zing of discomfort on the side of my left big toe as I powered up the endless incline, eager to get to the city and our first day's rest on the Camino. When I arrived at the *albergue* in Cardeñuela de Riopico and removed my socks, there it was. A fat, throbbing bulge that made my already ugly toe into something even more Gaudíesque. A good reminder of the dust from which I am made— and to which I will return.

The rocky ascent to the Matagrande Plain

There are, in fact, three kinds of suffering. The first kind is normally temporary—though its effects can last a long time in the form of misguided habits. It's largely caused by the idea that there is some pleasure we wished we had right now, but don't. It's an important form of suffering. We can master it—obtain our freedom from it, really—only over a long time of discipline, self-denial, and the development of right habits. Failure to deal effectively with this kind of suffering eventually leads to the third form of suffering, of which I'll have more to say soon.

But before there can be a third thing there must be a second thing. This is the kind of suffering that Job talks about when he asks:

> *Is not life on earth a drudgery,*
> *its days like those of a hireling?*
> *Like a slave who longs for the shade,*
> *a hireling who waits for wages,*
> *So I have been assigned months of futility,*
> *and troubled nights have been counted off for me. (Job 7:1–3)*

Job lost his family, his health, his worldly goods, and pretty much everything else during his terrible trials. Everyone experiences this kind of suffering in one form or another. To be human means to endure loss, hardship, bereavement, death, and the isolating pain of loneliness. It's just the way life is. Jesus himself—Jesus the human being—was sorely tempted by all the things that tempt me. And he knew suffering, and not just suffering on the cross. He cried real tears when his friend Lazarus died—even in the sure knowledge that God would raise him up again, and soon. St. Augustine reminds us:

We progress by means of trial.
No one knows himself except through trial.[1]

Of course, how we respond to this kind of suffering matters. And what also matters is how we respond when we encounter Job's lament in others, including others who are hard to like, much less love. If we get this wrong we really do damage to ourselves and to others around us. To overcome this kind of suffering requires a mature prayer life, and a mature prayer life is one where prayer is a habit. A life where we pray without ceasing. It is this kind of prayer life that casts our gaze toward Him whose mercy endures forever. Without this habit of prayer we are unlikely to look beyond the suffering of the moment to the gratitude that endures. And without gratitude for the blessings that come from the One in whose image and likeness we have been made, well, life really is just the sackcloth and ash that Job describes.

And there is a third kind of suffering to which I alluded earlier. This is the form of suffering that I want to focus on in this account of my pilgrimage on the Camino de Santiago. This is the kind of suffering that Dante Alighieri wrote about in *The Divine Comedy*.[2] The story opens with Dante describing the journey of his life. He finds himself in a dark forest where "the straightforward pathway had been lost." And he suddenly realizes this about his life: he does not know where he is, how he got there, or how he lost his way. Dante is basically saying, "I'm going in the wrong direction." And he is saying one additional thing. A critical thing. Maybe the most important thing. He admits that he was the one who lost the path. He does not claim that anyone else forced him from the true way. He doesn't point to his left or his right and shout, "He made me do it!" or "I was tricked. It's not my fault!" Good old Dante. He does a very hard thing. He tells the truth.

I was fired from my job in 2016. I cannot say for sure what led to my dismissal. College politics is a lot like the state of nature Thomas Hobbes described in his seventeenth-century *Leviathan*: "nasty and brutish."[3] I can

1. Augustine, "Office of Readings."
2. Alighieri, *Divine Comedy*, 1.
3. Hobbes, *Leviathan*, 289.

say without question that I was suffering as a result, and badly. I became angry and, despite my best efforts to the contrary, a bit depressed. Understandably, I viewed my dismissal as an injustice that wounded both my family and me. This anger put me on the wrong path. I grew frightened of where it might lead. I realized that if I didn't renounce this anger-filled way of life and the corrosive thoughts in which it was comfortably, deliciously, satisfyingly clothed I would spend my senior years—my "golden years"—as a bitter old man, a shriveled Golem-like version of myself.

Anger fills us with a sense of disordered righteousness. Anger feels wonderful, like a drug. We rage, we thunder with anger, and when we do we imagine ourselves to be armored in truth and justice. But it's all just foolish pride. Anger distorts our view of who we really are—and who others really are—just like a fun-house mirror. Yes, the path I was on—like the one Dante walked—had a sign that read, "*Abandon all hope, ye who enter here.*"

It slowly dawned on me that anger and the suffering it was causing did not have to be the final word. Suffering did not have to be the ultimate condition that defined my life. For just as surely as I could see Dante's warning flashing in big, neon colors, through the grace of a God who is too big for me to understand, I could also see another sign, this one from the prophet Jeremiah:

> *Stand by the earliest roads,*
> *ask the pathways of old,*
> *"Which is the way to good?" and walk it;*
> *thus you will find rest for yourselves. (Jer 6:16)*

I was at Mass one Sunday a few weeks after my job ended when my longtime friend, Joe, approached me and said, "I'm thinking of making a pilgrimage on the Camino de Santiago. Want to come?" The Camino had been a bucket list thing for me for a number of years. A mutual friend of ours, Fr. Steve Dudek, made the pilgrimage in 2006. Listening to his stories animated my thinking ever since. Did I want to go? Of course I did, but I recognized that I owed Carol a conversation, given the expense in dollars and time apart. Joe and I agreed that we would have coffee in two weeks to see where things stood.

My professional downfall was not hard only on me. Carol suffered terribly, and had a very difficult time going to work at the same college at which I worked. Even the stroll across campus to her office engendered powerful emotions. The fact that she supported me in such an unqualified way when I asked for her blessing on my pilgrimage is a gift for which I will always be grateful. Still, being absent from her for six weeks working out my anger while she languished at home is something that felt—and still feels—very selfish. Every step I took on my pilgrimage was filled with gratitude for her love.

The Camino de Santiago—literally "the Way of St. James"—is one of Christendom's oldest and most important pilgrimage journeys. Medieval pilgrims began their pilgrimage from wherever they lived and walked to the Cathedral of Santiago de Compostela in northwest Spain, where tradition claims the body of St. James the Apostle rests. While most modern pilgrims begin the journey in Sarria and only walk the last one hundred kilometers, Joe and I would meet pilgrims who began their walks in Germany, Austria, Hungary, the Netherlands, England, Ireland, and many other places.

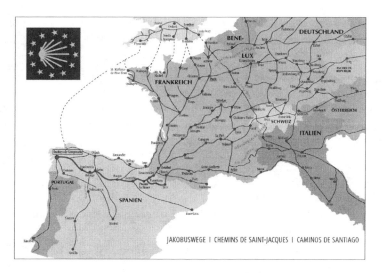

Joe and I would walk the "French Way," though there are many routes leading to Santiago de Compostela. (Manfred Zentgraf/Wikimedia Commons/CC BY 3.0)

Would we be walking to the actual burial site of St. James? I hadn't the faintest idea.[4] Martin Luther—no fan of pilgrimages—is said to have quipped, "There were twelve apostles, and eighteen of them are buried in

---

4. Andrew Boorde, a sixteenth-century physician-pilgrim was told by a resident priest to whom he confessed his sins that Charlemagne had removed all the relics of St. James to Toulouse many centuries before. Starkie, *Road to Santiago*, 54. This did not stop Pope Leo XIII from visiting Santiago de Compostela and officially certifying the remains. The pope described it in the bull *Omnipotens Deus*, published on November 1, 1884.

Spain."[5] What I do know—and this is my testimony—is that I hoped our five-hundred-mile walk would be a kind of long-form retreat that would teach me how to pray without ceasing, lead me to forgive my enemies, and help me to seek God's forgiveness for my own brokenness. I hoped to become a new creation on the Camino. I hoped to rediscover the True Way, and thus put behind me the third form of suffering.

Joe and I met for coffee two weeks after his fateful invitation. We stared at each other across the table, each of us waiting for the other to speak first. Finally, I simply blurted, "I'm in." "Me too," Joe responded.

Our resolve communicated, we got down to the work of planning for the pilgrimage. Joe is a retired electrical engineer who had important leadership responsibilities in a multinational firm. I was a college administrator. We were planners by instinct and habit. The planning we'd do for our pilgrimage would take several months. Joe researched and arranged for our transportation to St. Jean Pied-de-Port, France, and then home again from Santiago de Compostela. I took responsibility for determining a potential day-by-day itinerary. This eventually resulted in a spreadsheet that contained each day's starting point, ending point, total distance, options for walking a shorter or longer distance on any given day, special notes on what to see along the way, and an elevation map. We ordered our *credencial* or pilgrim passport, from the American Pilgrims on the Camino confraternity.[6] We joined an online Camino forum that connected us virtually to many hundreds of other pilgrims.[7] We would grow in gratitude for their generosity in sharing with us their experience and advice on a wide range of questions. Hoping to avoid the worst of the Spanish summer heat,[8] and with a desire to avoid the crowds, we settled on September 10 through October 21, 2016, as the dates for our pilgrimage. We had four months to get ready.

---

5. Hammond, *Luther.*

6. American Pilgrims on the Camino is one example of a pilgrim confraternity. Pilgrim guilds of this kind developed as early as the thirteenth century. Confraternities consist of former pilgrims. They tend to be national in nature, but they were originally founded as local guilds along the pilgrim routes whose members provided shelter, health care, and other forms of hospitality to those walking to Santiago de Compostela. Mullins, *Pilgrimage to Santiago,* 19.

7. https://www.caminodesantiago.me.

8. The British author Laurie Lee described afternoon Spanish heat as "silence, blinding white . . . destroyer, putrifier, scavenger of the hovels and breeder of swarming ills." Lee, *As I Walked,* 65.

**My *credencial* would eventually look like this
(scanned and uploaded by Jane023: June 2007,
public domain, via Wikimedia Commons)**

Joe and I have logged many miles backpacking with a wonderful group of friends over many years. One of the things we've learned is that we aren't as strong, as thin, or as durable as we once were. We determined that we would use the summer to achieve a level of fitness that would allow us to make the most of the pilgrimage. I lost thirty-seven pounds in the process. I cannot say if Joe lost weight or not, but I know that his fitness was up to the task we set before ourselves by the time we left for Spain. We walked all summer long, likely covering as many miles prowling the local countryside as we would once on Spanish soil. And we walked. And we walked some more. We usually walked alone, though a few times we got together and went for a fifteen-miler to see how we were likely to get along once faced with the real thing. I lifted weights and climbed the towering dunes near our home. Joe swam. Carol walked most of the long walks with me. God bless her for the company.

Our training for the Camino de Santiago included many miles along the Lake Michigan shoreline (Rosemtoubes, CC BY-SA 4.0 via Wikimedia Commons)

We also prepared spiritually for the pilgrimage. Our prayer lives deepened during that summer. One of the most significant places we would walk past on our Camino is *Cruz de Ferro* (Cross of Iron). This ancient landmark—the highest point of the Camino—is a place of special spiritual significance. Millions of pilgrims on their way to Santiago de Compostela have carried a stone from their home and left it at the foot of this very tall cross, offering the following prayer as they do:

> *O Lord, may the stone which I bring to this holy place be a sign of pilgrimage to Santiago. When I reach my final judgment, tip the balance of my life in favor of my good deeds. I lay down this token which I carry from home. Please forgive my sins and help me carry my burdens in life. Amen.*[9]

I picked up my stone while walking alone along the Lake Michigan shoreline. Each day as I prepared for my training walk I slipped it into my pocket as a reminder of the anger I hoped to lay at the foot of the ancient cross. It was my constant companion that summer, and an excellent reminder of why I was walking.

9. Ball, *Camino de Santiago.*

I looked forward to laying this down at Cruz de Ferro

Joe and I met several times to name the anxieties we had as the pilgrimage approached. Did we have the physical stamina to walk five hundred miles? Would our health hold up? Would we become homesick for our families during such a long time away from home? Would the prayer intentions we carried with us to Spain find fertile ground on the Camino? How would our patience with each other—and our friendship—be tested during thirty-two days of little else but walking? What didn't we know that we wished we did know? Naming these anxieties turned out to be helpful preparation. The questions we asked ourselves turned out to be the right questions, though of course we couldn't know that at the time. The advice offered by William Wey, the fifteenth-century pilgrim to Santiago de Compostela and Jerusalem, seemed like a good guide for our own pilgrimage: *Si fore vis sapiens sex serva quae tibi mondo. Quid loqueris, et ubi, de quo, cui, quomodo, quando:*[10]

> *If your life would keep from slips,*
> *Five things observe with care;*
> *Of whom you speak, to whom you speak,*
> *And how, and when, and where.*

---

10. Roxburghe et al., *Itineraries*, 18.

Ten daily trips up steps to the top of the wooded dunes—with a backpack—proved to be good training for the mountains we would climb in France and Spain (hakkun, CC BY-SA 3.0 via Wikimedia Commons)

Eventually the day for our departure arrived. While all seemed to be in readiness I couldn't overcome a kind of pensiveness of mood and mindset. This is a familiar aspect of my personality. I'm frequently nervous in the hours before leaving on a trip—as if my only source of happiness is to be found someplace else. Still, I had prepared my body. My spirit—while always a work in progress—was well attended to, and no amount of delay or additional preparation would substitute for the benefits of the pilgrimage itself. My backpack had been filled, emptied, rebalanced, and reweighed a dozen times. All forty-nine items had been carefully weighed, prioritized, and selected for their ability to serve multiple purposes. My worries as I sat in my living room waiting for Joe to arrive for our trip to the airport were largely in the category of "things you can't change." The predicted hot weather in Spain. The complicated travel schedule over the next twenty-four hours. I just needed to let it all go, mindful of St. Ambrose Barlow's advice (whose feast day coincided with our departure day): "Let them fear that have anything to lose which they are unwilling to part with."[11]

---

11. See https://www.st-catherines-didsbury.co.uk/st-ambrose.html.

The Beginning

Dishonest Cabbies and Carsick Pilgrims

J OE and I were both experienced international travelers. Still, I am no fan of the long airplane rides and the serial airport hopping that is part and parcel of journeys like the one we embarked upon as we set out from the Gerald Ford International Airport in Grand Rapids. Our route took us first to Chicago, and then on the long flight to Madrid. We transferred there for a short hop to Pamplona, where we took a taxi to the bus station to board the *autobús* for the ride over the Pyrenees to St. Jean Pied-de-Port, France.

The landscape from the airplane window as we prepared to land in Pamplona was the color of a mud puddle as harvested wheat fields as far as the eye could see rolled in shades of tan in the late summer sunlight. Our first impressions of Pamplona were a far cry from the *Ferminista*-throbbing frenzy of the guidebooks.[1] It being a Sunday afternoon in the off-season, the place seemed less asleep than comatose.

1. The running of the bulls for which Pamplona is famous takes place during the Feast of San Fermín. The city goes wild with revelers during this time—many of whom don traditional white pants and shirts with the red sash and neckerchief of the *Ferminista*. See Instituto de Turismo de España, "San Fermín," https://www.spain.info/en/

Our Pamplona cabbie was a savvy fellow. He quickly identified us as pilgrims. Bewildered Americans speaking broken Spanish carrying backpacks and trekking poles are not hard to identify in Pamplona. Through a bit of sign language, Google Translate, and sputtering English he explained that, this being Sunday, no busses would be leaving the station today. "But we have a prepaid ticket to St. Jean Pied-de-Port," we explained in worried voices. "*No se. No autobús hoy. Es Domingo.*" (I don't know. No bus today. It's Sunday.) The next ten minutes were spent in contingency planning for how we would get over the mountains and into France so we could start walking. Would we have to pay this taxi driver a big fat fare to take us there? Would we have to eat the money we'd already spent on the bus ticket? The prepaid bus ticket turned out to be worth the expense. The bus to St. Jean was waiting in the station as the taxi pulled in. Thank you very much, Mr. Dishonest Cabbie.

In his First Letter to the Thessalonians,[2] St. Paul admonishes the church there to "pray without ceasing." A long airplane ride followed by a five-week walk is a good way to practice this spiritual exercise. As the plane lifted off earlier in the day I whispered a prayer that the letters I had mailed to a number of people with whom I was angry would land on receptive hearts, and that the friendships I once enjoyed with these people could be restored once I returned from the pilgrimage. These were hard letters to write, and they took most of the summer for me to locate just the right words. Was I mad at these folks? Volcanically so. But I knew that I would have to take the first step in inviting a renewal of a relationship for my own healing to begin. And I had to face the very real possibility that I'd done something to deserve their enmity. None of us knows ourselves as well as we think, and I had to admit that as I offered forgiveness and sought theirs as well. I was not sure how the letters would be received. Would the recipients scoff at this effort? Might they also be angry with me, and would the letters further inflame their anger? I just did not know.

Those on my "naughty list" were not the only people to whom I mailed a letter as I walked out the door of my apartment for the last time in six weeks. People in my life who were seriously ill or in the process of dying would also hear from me as my pilgrimage unfolded. I let each of them know where I would be on the Camino when I offered a prayer for their healing. Some have now died, some are healed, and some continue to struggle. I

---

calendar/fiestas-san-fermin/.

2. 1 Thess 5:17.

hope all knew—and still know—how important they were to me. Finally, I wrote letters to a number of close personal friends. We so infrequently thank our friends for the gift of their friendship. My pilgrimage seemed like a good opportunity to correct that fault.

We met some interesting fellow pilgrims in our travels on Day 1, though one in particular served to raise our already jet-lagged anxieties a bit. Santiago from Brazil was easily recognizable as we scanned the Madrid airport waiting lounge. Pilgrims to St. James are hard to miss. We all share the same uniform, just like Catholic school children. Scallop shells, hiking clothes, backpacks, and floppy hats are the order of the day. We formed several impressions in the blink of an eye after introducing ourselves to Santiago. To say that he seemed ultra-organized is an understatement. Keep in mind that in these early hours of our pilgrimage everything we saw and heard had an oversized effect on how we were imagining the next six weeks. Santiago got us wondering if we were really ready for this. He was tall and carried himself with military bearing. Where I was soft and vulnerable he was hard-edged and sculpted. He carried himself with an easy confidence that practically screamed, "Five hundred miles? No big deal!" I found myself sucking in my gut and standing up straighter in his presence, like a pilgrim version of trying out for the junior varsity football team. But what started to get Joe and me more than a bit freaked out was Santiago's T-shirt. It was obviously custom-made just for this occasion. On the right breast where one might normally find a company's logo, Santiago had listed in bright red letters his name, the Brazilian flag, the year of his pilgrimage, and his blood type. His blood type?! None of the guidebooks warned us to do this. We began to worry that if we fell off the mountain tomorrow Spain's Finest would not know our blood type. Would we die from a bad blood transfusion on this trip? Do pilgrims normally require blood transfusions as the price for developing their spiritual fitness? Santiago was eventually joined by a fellow countryman with a blood type we failed to note. They chatted comfortably and confidently in their native Portuguese, while Joe and I stole furtive glances across the heat-rippled tarmac.

St. James the Apostle, pray for us! (Jojojoe/Wikimedia Commons/CC BY 3.0)

We spotted other pilgrims in various places through which we transited. I sat next to a sniffling, face-lifted Scottish woman on the Madrid leg of the journey. She was coming from Los Angeles to walk the Camino, but also planned to buy an apartment on Tenerife, where she once lived and owned a restaurant with a Spanish man to whom she was married "who didn't quite work out." Another woman from California chatted to us in the airport. She was flying to Santiago de Compostela to join friends with whom she would walk the last 110 kilometers from Sarria. The Pamplona bus station was alive with pilgrims. Grace from New Zealand, Mike from Oregon, and Cathy from Florida kept us company while we waited to board the bus. Cathy's bad hips had kept her from starting several months earlier. "I just retired. I've done the kid thing, the mom thing, the money thing, the house thing, and the job thing. Now it's finally time for the Cathy thing." Amen to that.

We boarded the bus and headed northeast toward France and St. Jean Pied-de-Port. The hills were gently rolling as the bus proceeded first through Pamplona's suburbs and then into farm country. After perhaps twenty minutes the bus seemed to tilt upward like an airplane leaving the runway as we began the climb into and through the Pyrenees. The views from the window were staggeringly beautiful and revealed a landscape seemingly vertical. I felt myself breathing a bit harder just thinking of walking over those mountains as we made the return trip from France back through Pamplona and then across the rest of Spain. I hoped my summer training was enough. While writing my notes as the bus swerved left and then right as it steadily climbed, a carsick pilgrim vomited lavishly in the bus lavatory. Terrific.

Arriving in hot, sunny Pamplona proved a shocking contrast to our departure from familiar West Michigan

The view from the bus window was sobering. We'd soon be walking over these mountains (Benh LIEU SONG/Wikimedia Commons/CC BY 2.0)

The bus pulled up to the bus stop on the outskirts of St. Jean Pied-de-Port two hours after leaving Pamplona. As Joe and I stepped off and retrieved our backpacks from the luggage bin we felt both exhausted from our long trip and jittery with excitement to begin our pilgrimage. But we planned to spend the night in St. Jean to get some rest before we headed out toward the valley through which Charlemagne had retreated from Spain after bloodying the nose of the occupying Moors. We set off in search of the Beilari *gite* (as pilgrim hostels are called in France). We had no idea where it was. We simply followed the rest of the pilgrims who got off the bus and they led us to the main street—Rue de la Citadelle. Fortunately for us, it was a short street and we located the *albergue* easily. We were met by *hospitaleros* Joselu and Jakline, who welcomed us warmly and provided a supper of vegetable soup, bread, wine, and cheese. The meal was a group affair shared by other pilgrims sharing the house that night. One of the pilgrims with whom we shared our dinner—an Austrian—started his Camino in Vienna months earlier. He walked over the top of Mt. Blanc—Europe's highest peak—through all of France, over the Pyrenees, across Spain, ending at the Atlantic Ocean at Cape Finisterre.[3] Then he turned around and rode his bike back the other way. When we met him he was one-third of the way home. The sheer athleticism of his pilgrimage was both inspiring and a bit intimidating.

After dinner we checked in at the Pilgrim Office across the street from the *albergue*. The volunteers were helpful and encouraging, providing us with written materials offering advice on routes over the mountains and pilgrim etiquette for the herds of sheep regularly encountered (don't bother the sheep, step off the path to allow the sheep to pass, don't bother the shepherds, etc., etc.). After getting our *credencial* stamped, we were ready for bed, to which we went without any further delay, exhausted but grateful that our pilgrimage had finally begun.

The Low Road

We tossed and turned much of the night with jet lag. Though I had no problems falling asleep, staying asleep wasn't as easy. The room was too warm and stuffy. My fellow pilgrims snuffled in their bunks just loud enough to keep me awake. I probably slept more than I imagined, but it seemed like a very long night. Around 6:30 a beautiful melody began to fill the house. It started off slow and low, but grew over perhaps the next fifteen minutes. It was a lovely way for the *hospitaleros* to gently awaken us.

---

3. The town of Fisterra is located on Cape Finisterre. *Fisterra* is a Galician place name, while *Finisterre* is Spanish. All of this gets a bit confusing. The bottom line is that both names are more or less interchangeable. I think.

This morning would be our first experience with "waking up, packing up, fueling up, and moving out." The morning *albergue* routines required more mental energy on that first day then would be the case as our pilgrimage continued westward. I remember thinking that I'd be glad when they become more habitual. *Albergue* quarters are usually cramped, and Beilari's were no exception. It was easy to jostle each other as we bent over to fill packs, tie shoes, and make the usual morning time adjustments. Eventually I would learn to pack up the night before so that upon waking I could simply step from my bunk into the *albergue's* common area, thus giving myself more room to maneuver while making less noise in consideration of those pilgrims who weren't yet awake.

Our first *sello* (stamp) from St. Jean Pied-de-Port

Our hosts provided us with a self-serve breakfast in the Beilari's dining room. It was a dimly lit place. The sun had not yet risen, so we had to be a bit careful to avoid spills and accidents at the crowded common table. The pilgrims—so convivial at dinner last night—were more sober this morning. There seemed to be a kind of collective anxiety that hung over us, since for most of us this was to be Day 1 of the Big Walk. Unlike Joe and me, most of our fellow travelers would be tackling the Napoleon Route over the mountains and walking all the way to Roncesvalles by the end of the day. Joe and I had decided before we left Holland that we would break the typical first day up into two portions, walking only as far as Valcarlos. This route also had the advantage of following the Rio Luzaide through the valley, making for much less climbing on the first day. There would be a very steep section the next day, but it would be significantly shorter than the Napoleon Route that most at the table would take.

The day was predicted to be a scorcher, with temperatures in the upper nineties Fahrenheit. Given my recent history with kidney stones, I was more than a bit anxious about staying adequately hydrated—just one more thing to add to the list of traveling anxieties.

Backpacks ready and shoelaces tied, we were finally ready to start walking around 7:30. This was later than most mornings on the Camino, but we knew we had a relatively short walk, and our morning routine would eventually grow more efficient, refined, and reflexive as we gained experience. As we took our first of what would be more than one million steps to the Atlantic Ocean, I was cognizant of how important the Camino has been for more than a thousand years. The pilgrimage to St. James is asserted to be the key to understanding the medieval period with its decidedly non-twenty-first-century worldviews.[4] There are those who theorize that the very idea of "Europe" was an unvisualized concept prior to the establishment of the Camino de Santiago.[5] Walking through all of this history would be a privilege.

We headed for the *Porte d'Espagne* (Door to Spain) past the fourteenth-century Gothic church, Notre-Dame-du-Bout-du-Pont. The walk to the village gate took only five minutes, but in that short time we were able to traverse most of the length of St. Jean Pied-de-Port. Edwin Mullins, the British author, art critic, and television personality, has, with a clever turn of phrase, described St. Jean Pied-de-Port as "a town with a great deal of make-up and not much face."[6] While Mr. Mullins offers many insightful observations in his 1974 book, his pen owes this picturesque Basque village an apology. St. Jean is thoroughly charming. Were Joe and I not so eager to begin our pilgrimage, it would have been very pleasant indeed to linger there awhile, strolling alongside La Nive de Beherobie as it winds lazily through the town between ancient white houses festooned with colorful window planters. Really, Mr. Mullins. Sometimes a place that looks like a nice place is, in fact, a nice place. Well, perhaps we should not expect too much magnanimity from a person who admits that he "would have made a rotten pilgrim in any age."

---

4. Kendall, *Medieval Pilgrims*, 29.

5. Dudek, personal communication (2018).

6. Mullins, *Pilgrimage to Santiago*, 87.

St. Jean Pied-de-Port (A1AA1A/Wikimedia Commons CC BY 4.0)

Our route took us through rolling farm country flanked on both sides by mountains of increasing height and steepness. The morning was quiet, and we had the one-lane road mostly to ourselves, not counting the cows, sheep, chickens and other barnyard inhabitants that mooed, bleated, and clucked in greeting as we strolled past. Though we broke into sun-filled glades from time to time, the combination of soaring hills and roadside trees kept us well-shaded from the rising late summer sun. We did encounter one other pilgrim. Victoria from Italy biked past us until the road grew hilly and arduous. She dismounted—red in the face—and gave a sheepish look as we caught up with her and she freely admitted, "I'm not really much of a biker." After wishing her well we strolled on.

We stopped after seven kilometers for our first official pilgrim *cafe con leche* break at about 9:30 in the village of Arneguy. These refreshment stops would become part of our pilgrimmy habits. It was very pleasant indeed to wake up and greet the day with an hour or two of walking before splurging on one of Spain's greatest gifts to walkers—a rich jolt of espresso calmed by thick, warm milk. Sometimes I would pay, and sometimes Joe would pay. We tried to keep our out-of-pocket expenses equal for any given day of the pilgrimage. While we were enjoying our coffee Victoria came limping into the village. Her husband, Leonardo, poured her into their car, put the bike up on the rack, and the two of them headed off for presumably flatter country. I hoped Victoria would be able to continue her Camino as she desired.

Our caffeine requirements met, we pushed on up the increasing declivitous valley toward Valcarlos. The Camino took us on a mix of wooded paths, country lanes, and even along the shoulder of the paved highway N-135 for a while. We walked through the hamlet of Óndarolle about eleven kilometers after St. Jean. Like many Spanish villages through which we would walk, Óndarolle seemed to be a ghost town—almost like an Old West Hollywood movie set with false fronts on the buildings and no people whatsoever. The houses seemed well-maintained and the hamlet pleasant enough. Where were the people?

Heading west (and up) from St. Jean to Valcarlos

We arrived at Valcarlos as the church bells sounded 11:00. Though the heat was quickly building to a fierce intensity, we toyed with the idea of continuing to Roncesvalles. There was plenty of time. We decided to stick with our plan of an easy first day, knowing that the rest of the way to Roncesvalles is vertically challenging and respirationally rigorous.

We had some trouble locating the town's lone *albergue*. The guidebook was murky about the precise location, though it did indicate unhelpfully that the key "may be" in the municipal building. There was nobody on the street to whom we could ask directions except for an elderly man limping down the sidewalk leaning heavily on a walking stick. When I asked him in my very best Spanish where the *albergue* was located he looked at me like I was an alien new to the planet and responded with a barely audible *como*? Well, he was worth a try. I smiled in appreciation for his time and moved on to a building that looked like it could be city hall. The first-floor lobby was empty, so I made my way up the stairs to the second floor. After knocking on several doors of apparently abandoned offices I finally found a woman who turned out to be very helpful, though it took a few minutes of twenty-questions for me to reach this conclusion. "*Hola. Dónde está el albergue?*" I inquired in perfectly accented Navarrese Spanish. She responded in either Spanish or Basque, though I couldn't really tell because it was coming at me so fast. I picked up a single word: *abajo* (down or underneath). She wrote a door code on a post-it note and handed it to me and repeated *abajo*. When I looked at her with the dull, vacant expression of a lobotomy patient that clearly communicated that *abajo* was not going to get me to the *albergue*, she very helpfully stood up from her desk and walked us to the *albergue*, which was right next door in the lower level of the town school. Ah ha! *Abajo*!

Valcarlos was sleepy in the hazy Spanish heat
(Rodelar/Wikimedia Commons CC BY 4.0)

We were the first pilgrims to arrive at the *albergue*, so we had our choice of beds. After showering and handwashing our sweaty clothes, we found a shady spot and ate our lunch. Since we had plenty of time, we explored the *supermercado* (which wasn't too "super"—just a small shop selling everything from various groceries to spark plugs to duct tape) to investigate food options for cooking dinner. We bought ingredients for a salad, chorizo, Basque cheese, pears, and lemon cream cookies. Yum.

After a nap we strolled over to the village church. It was locked—something we would encounter far too often as we continued our Camino—but we walked up the hill behind the church and strolled through the cemetery. Being from the flatlands of Michigan, the views from the heights above the town to the soaring mountains across the valley struck me as majestically stunning. Sheep grazed on the hillside, and we could hear an occasional cowbell drift across the heat-rippled spaces. And it was very hot—ninety-eight degrees Fahrenheit. Heading back to the shade of the *albergue* we encountered three Italian middle-aged *peregrinas* looking for directions to Roncesvalles. They were hot and tired already with the hottest, longest, steepest part of the walk to go. We shared our map with them and they continued. I hope they made it OK.

Around 4:00 we were joined in the *albergue* by four pilgrims. John was from Vermont and Britta and Marion were from Germany. Reynard was French.[7] They were exhausted—nearly half dead—from the heat. Britta and Marion had to take a cab from Arneguy because they were too wrung out to continue by foot. John was a yakker of Herculean fecundity. Would. Not. Be. Quiet. When not talking to us (about any and all subjects, from his history of leg infections to standards used in the adjudication of Medicare claims) he simply talked to himself. Fortunately, he was a pleasant fellow.

Reynard the Fox Equipped for His Pilgrimage (Allart van Everdingen – Reynard the Fox – Reynard Equipped for His Pilgrimage – 1982.179.34 – Cleveland Museum of Art. tif (Wikimedia/(CC0 1.0)

7. I cannot assert with complete confidence that Reynard's name was not actually *Ronald*. His English was very spotty and heavily accented. When he introduced himself he told me his name was "Ronald—like the fox." The fox to which I think he refers is called Reynard, and has a long literary presence back to medieval times.

During the pilgrimage I'd continue to pray the *Liturgy of the Hours* as I had for the past year or so. Compline is the evening prayer, and after reading this helpful, encouraging prayer, I called it a day, grateful for a good start to our pilgrimage. As I lay in my bed in the darkening bunkroom, I could feel some of the traveling worries gently fade as I recalled Auden's advice in his poem "Atlantis," hoping "the Ancient of Days" would "lift me up in the light of his countenance."[8]

Up and Over

Just like my nocturnal restlessness in St. Jean Pied-de-Port, the Valcarlos *albergue* offered only intermittent sleep, with tossing and turning the norm. Is this what I would have to look forward to for the next month? I certainly hoped not. I tend to be particularly sensitive to jet lag, and I hoped that once I fully adjusted to the time zone in which I found myself that sleep uninterrupted would be my happy report.

Valcarlos is called Luzaide by its native Basques

"Cooking breakfast" involved heating water for an instant coffee and tearing open the cellophane wrapper of a grocery store muffin. While enjoying this culinary low point of the day a uniformed village worker-cum-*hospitalero* for this municipal *albergue* came in to collect our fees, stamp our *credencials*, and generally check to make sure all was well. The sky was lightening beautifully over the Pyrenees as we fumbled our gear into our packs with unpracticed hands, trying our best not to disturb the

8. Auden, "Atlantis."

sleep of Britta and Marion, for whom the first day's exertions were likely still exacting a toll. Both were rather stout, and the rigors of long-distance walking over steep terrain left them utterly knackered. I found myself admiring them for their commitment to doing their best despite circumstances, physical and meteorological.

"Uptight Rich" was fully present on this beautiful morning. Thunderstorms were predicted all afternoon, and I worried about being caught in the open on top of the mountain in such weather. The Camino is generally a safe and relatively gentle place to walk. That said, if there are horror stories told around evening pilgrim campfires they are of death and danger in the mountains—mountains we would be climbing that day. We only had eight miles to walk, and we hoped we'd beat the bad weather.

Our walk out of Valcarlos was pleasant. My feet and legs felt pretty good with little soreness or evidence of other orthopedic impediment. Just beyond the village limits we passed a garden arrayed with scarecrows in the form of mannequin heads mounted on poles. I am not sure if this was effective in keeping the crows out of the corn, but it gave Joe and me a start as we imagined rough medieval justice meted out in this little-considered corner of Spain.

The route out of Valcarlos took us on a 3.7-kilometer stroll through the hamlet of Gañecoleta, after which the Camino ducked into the shade of the woods. The path up to that point had a gentle upward slope sufficient to warm the legs and cast the eyes upward. But suddenly the earth began to tip, and for the next eight kilometers we seemed to be climbing a ladder ever upward. I could count my heartbeats in my ears as my lungs filled and emptied like a smith's bellows. The footpath was mostly dirt and leaf-litter with few rocky places. As we climbed toward the Ibañeta Pass at 1057m (3,467 ft) I found myself thankful for all those stairs I'd climbed in the months leading to the pilgrimage.

Eventually the path leveled a bit as the trees thinned and the summit came into view. We found ourselves at a scenic overview of the stunning valley guarded by the rugged shoulders of the Pyrenees. A monument to Roland memorializes his horn blast alerting Charlemagne that his rearguard was defeated by the Moors (though most credible historical records report that it was the Basques that defeated Roland in retaliation for Charlemagne's destruction of Pamplona's walls—and his liberties with Pamplona's maidens—during an earlier campaign).

Painting by Wolf von Bibra (1862–1922) of the Battle of Roncevaux Pass from
The Song of Roland based on print by "A Closs" (Wikimedia Commons CC BY 4.0)

We met two Spaniards about our age on a motorcycle tour at the
Ibañeta overlook. One spoke pretty good English and engaged us in conversation. He asked our views about the US presidential campaign, which was
then in full, raging, free-falling, mudslinging, America-at-its-worst mode.
This would be a common conversation theme for the remainder of our
pilgrimage, with people from all over the world enraptured with American politics in much the same way that Americans are manic about the
British royal family. Our Spanish interlocutor told us how much he envied
America because, in his words, "You are so unified." Joe and I gave each
other a sideways glance and, as if our thoughts were joined in a Vulcan
mind meld, wondered how to respond to this seemingly ridiculous assertion. "Well, we're really not that unified, you know." I responded gently, so
as not to offend. "Oh, believe me, you Americans are very unified compared
to us Spaniards. I am very jealous. Spain is always spinning and trying to
throw off parts of itself. You are new here. Just wait until you finish your
pilgrimage—you'll see."

In the end, of course, he was right. Spanish politics are hard for Americans to comprehend. Perhaps they are hard for all non-Spaniards to comprehend. The memories of the Spanish civil war are still fresh and vividly alive among the people—especially the older folks. It had not been that many years that Spain transitioned—in halting, challenging ways—from the dictatorship of Generalissimo Francisco Franco to the constitutional monarchy of the present era. It has only been a democracy in a widely accepted sense of the term since 1978. Spain has seventeen autonomous regions, many of which have distinct cultures and co-official languages. When Americans hear "Spain," they imagine a modern, consolidated nation occupying the larger part of the Iberian Peninsula and exercising an important influence in European—indeed global—affairs. When Spaniards hear the same word, they are more likely to think of their Galician, Navarrese/Basque, or Castilian homeland, its culture, local language, and potentially independent political aspirations. We never met a Barcelonan who claimed to be from Spain—all were self-described Catalans.[9] People from the northeast of Spain claimed to be Basque, not Spanish. Signs in Castilla y León frequently had either Castilla or León spray painted out of the picture.

A common theme on our walk through Spain

9. Catalonian president Carles Puigdemont would eventually go on the run, dodging arrest by Spanish authorities on charges of sedition and rebellion for sponsoring a plebiscite which, if approved, would have established Catalonia as an independent nation. Wilson, "Ex-Catalan Leader."

After cresting the summit, we had a gentle downhill stroll along a lovely forest path toward the village of Roncesvalles, at which we arrived at 11:15. We were glad to arrive early, for the weather began to turn from blue skies with the occasional wispy cloud to a leaden grayness. The temperature was thirty degrees Fahrenheit cooler than yesterday—with a stiff, chilling wind and intermittent drizzle. The Dutch *hospitalero* told us that pilgrims would not be admitted to the *albergue* until 1:00, so we had time to munch on leftovers from last night's supper while we had a look around the monastery grounds. The *albergue* was ancient and huge, accommodating nearly four hundred pilgrims. The wing in which we were assigned our beds had been renovated with modern conveniences, but the old section that shelters the overflow of pilgrims was a simple stone hall with soaring ceilings and a decidedly medieval feel. Many Spaniards begin the Camino in Roncesvalles rather than in St. Jean Pied-de-Port. A twelfth-century poem explains well the purpose of the Roncesvalles *albergue*, which was established as a hospital for pilgrims surviving the arduous journey over the Pyrenees:

> *Porta patet omnibus, infirmis et sanis*
> *Non solum Catholicis verum et paganis*
> *Judeis, hereticis, otiosis, vanis . . .*
> *(The door is open to all, to sick and healthy*
> *Not only to Catholics, but to pagans, Jews,*
> *heretics, vagabonds, and frivolous . . .)*[10]

The Roncesvalles *albergue* was, in ancient days, one of the most hospitable of the pilgrim accommodations along the road to Santiago de Compostela. At many hospices the most pilgrims could hope for was a roof, a pile of straw on which to sleep, some water, and enough bread to sustain them. Anything we moderns might think of as medical services were unlikely to be provided, though pilgrims who died while in the care of the hospice could count on a dignified burial. At Roncesvalles, however, travelers who just climbed the Pyrenees would find an actual bed in either a male or female dormitory, have their feet washed, receive hearty, nourishing meals, and be invited to participate in the full range of religious services.[11]

10. Vázquez de Parga et al., *Peregrinaciones*, 101.
11. Mullins, *Pilgrimage to Santiago*, 72.

The distinctive *sello* of the ancient *albergue* at Roncesvalles

We chatted with a Brit while munching on our lunch in the monastery courtyard. He arrived over the Napoleon Route just after us. He took the Valcarlos route the year before and said it was a much more challenging walk! So much for our planning, though it encouraged us that the training we'd done was paying off. Reynard/Ronald from France, who shared the Valcarlos *albergue* with us, left at the same time as we did that morning, but arrived in Roncesvalles about two hours later, perhaps because he pulled a cart with his pack. I imagine that this must slow him considerably as he navigated the narrow, bouldery forest trails. I think he had a bad back. His system was ingenious, and allowed him to enjoy long-distance hiking despite his inability to carry a pack. If what Joe and I were doing was "backpacking," what should we call Reynard's experience? "Carting?" "Two-wheeling?" "Pulling?"

The downtime that afternoon provided an opportunity for reflection on the purpose of my pilgrimage. The "Jesus Prayer," first described in Luke's gospel and later the special devotional of the fourth-century Desert Fathers, has a special place in the Eastern Orthodox tradition, including pilgrims seeking a closer connection with God. *Oh Lord, draw me closer to you, and be merciful to me, a sinner* has been a helpful prayer to keep me focused on why I'm doing this pilgrimage. It was frequently on my lips during those times when Joe and I walked separately. In a similar way, the plea of the pilgrims Jesus encountered on the road to Emmaus was efficacious medicine for me on that day: *Stay with us, for it is nearly evening and the day is almost over.*[12] Like them, I hoped that my encounter with Him while walking The Way would cause my heart to burn.

We eventually checked into the *albergue*, booked our shared pilgrim dinner at the adjacent restaurant, and collected our *sello*. The bunks were arranged in cubicles of four. It was fun to meet (while the skies opened and rain poured down in torrents) elderly Morgan from Maastricht in the Netherlands, who shared our bunk cubicle, and tell them that we were from Holland in the United States. We were also impressed by the young couple—assigned beds just down the row from ours—who were making the pilgrimage with their five-month-old baby. More impressive is that they'd already walked five hundred miles with her since July, when they began their Camino in LePuy, France![13] He pulled a rig similar to Reynard/Ronald's with all their gear, while she carried the baby.

Joe and I sat next to a young Liverpudlian at the pilgrim's dinner. He had walked the Camino five times, in addition to a twelve-hundred-kilometer hike through Hungary. He had a doctorate, but seemed to lack a sense of vocation or calling. He described being fed up with the corporate-government structure of society, and seemed quite jaded. Religion, he asserted, is a big part of the problem. His views saddened me, for they reflect a kind of skepticism that understands freedom as being anything you may wish to do. Still, I was glad for the encounter. This fellow reminded me of the enormity of the task that educators have to help our youth discern vocations, understand themselves as existing not only (or even principally) for themselves, and to implant a sense of hope for the future.

We finished the day with an evening Mass at the monastery church—La Iglesia de Santa María. At the conclusion of the liturgy the priest offered the traditional blessing for all pilgrims. We were called up to the altar, where the priest prayed over us the pilgrim prayer of St. James:[14]

> *O God, who brought your servant Abraham*
> *out of the land of the Chaldeans,*
> *protecting him in his wandering across the desert,*

---

12. Luke 24:29.

13. Le Puy was an important medieval Marian pilgrimage destination, along with being one of the four traditional French jumping-off points for the Road to St. James. Cartwright reports that four popes made pilgrimage to Le Puy. So did Charlemagne, various kings, and several saints. Joan of Arc's mother came to pray for her daughter's "strange, wonderful, and tragic mission." Cartwright, *Catholic Shrines*, 90.

14. St. James Cathedral, "Pilgrim Prayers," https://www.stjames-cathedral.org/camino/prayer.aspx.

*we ask that you watch over us, your servants, as we walk in the love of your
name to Santiago de Compostela.*

Be for us our companion on the walk,
Our guide at the crossroads,
Our breath in our weariness,
Our protection in danger,
Our home (albergue) on the Camino,
Our shade in the heat,
Our light in the darkness,
Our consolation in our discouragements,
And our strength in our intentions.

*So that with your guidance we may arrive safe and sound at the
end of the road and enriched with grace and virtue we return safely
to our homes filled with joy. In the name of Jesus Christ our Lord,
Amen. Apostle Santiago, pray for us. Santa Maria, pray for us.*

It was a moving experience—one which provided a realization that
we were not alone on this pilgrimage. Indeed, we were surrounded by like-
minded fellow travelers—travelers who were walking the same physical
and spiritual path as us. This was a terrific encouragement.

As we strolled around the church after Mass, we got our first glimpse
of St. James in one of the three forms in which he is depicted along the
Camino—indeed, through much of the Spanish-speaking world. Santiago
Apostol—St. James the Apostle—is the instantiation of the contemporary
and friend of Jesus that we read about in the Scriptures. This is the James
who was the brother of John, both of whom were the sons of Zebedee—the
biblical "Sons of Thunder." Often barefoot, he sometimes carries a staff and
is usually shown with a scroll in his left hand. *Santiago Peregrino*—St. James
the Pilgrim—wears a long cape and a hat turned up in front as protection
against the elements. His staff has a gourd that serves as a primitive water
vessel. A small satchel (scrip) slung over his shoulder with a leather strap
carries necessities for travel along the road. He is easily identified by the
scallop shell attached to his hat. Sometimes he is positively festooned with
scallop shells on hat, scrip, and cape. *Santiago Matamoros*—St. James the
Moor-Slayer—is the product of a legend in which St. James was seen miraculously mowing down Moorish occupiers during the mythical Battle of
Clavijo. This depiction of James has had tremendous durability in Spanish-
speaking culture, and has influenced the naming of settlements and family
names both in the Old and New Worlds. *Santiago Matamoros* was the

Patron Saint of Spain until he was replaced in 1760—at the insistence of Pope Clement XIII—by the Immaculate Conception. *Santiago Apostol* was installed as patron of the Spanish people at that time.[15]

At Roncesvalles we have our first encounter with St. James in his *Santiago Peregrino* persona

Santiago Matamoros vanquishing the Moors in Burgos Cathedral (Sustiputo/WikimediaCC BY-SA 3.0 ES)

15. St. Teresa of Ávila was a favorite of some to be installed as Patroness of Spain. In the end, the permanency of St. James in the Spanish imagination was too strong to unseat him from this honored position.

790 Kilometers. Oh My.

We woke to cloudy, threatening skies and temperatures that were forty degrees Fahrenheit cooler than just two days ago. We could see our breath as we made final adjustments to shoelaces and backpacks in the monastery courtyard. It was still dark when we set off at 7:00, but there was a long line of pilgrims we could follow, so we did not worry about getting lost. A road sign reading "Santiago de Compostela 790" greeted us as we stepped onto the trail. I will admit to feeling a bit daunted by such a big number printed in such a large font in such a prominent position so close to the pilgrim path. If road signs could laugh and smirk, this one would serve as a model.

Miles to go. Miles to go.

The first forty minutes of westward progress took us along a misty forest track. Our guidebook informed us that nine women were executed by the Inquisition in the sixteenth century for allegedly practicing witchcraft in this forest. Thanks guidebook. As if it was not creepy enough stumbling along in the murky darkness with every cracking twig setting the imagination a-reeling!

After about four kilometers we left the haunted forest and wandered onto the main street of Burguete—population 290. Burguete has a fire department that serves as the first source of help for pilgrims in need of rescue on the Napoleon Route over the Pyrenees. The Camino is not a dangerous walking route. It contains few hazards for the sensible pilgrim—though it should be noted that common sense is normally distributed in the population, with quite a few folks falling well below the mean. Perhaps this fact accounted for the following medieval pilgrim hymn:

You who are going to Santiago,
I humbly beg you
Make no haste:
Go your way gently.
Alas! How the poor sick folk
Are in great discomfort!
For many men and women
By the wayside are dead.[16]

There was a bar on the corner and, feeling a need for refueling, we took off our packs and enjoyed a ham and cheese croissant with *cafe con leche* for breakfast. Yum. The sky was brightening as we finished breakfast and rejoined the Camino. The Roncesvalles *albergue* had spit a steady stream of pilgrims onto the road. I began chatting with a tall Italian fellow who was about my age. Guido was from Genoa, and this was his first Camino. He was a very nice guy to pass the time with as we made our way through the village, out onto the farm lane that took us into the countryside, and across the Rio Irati toward Espinal. He apologized constantly for his English, but he was more competent than he gave himself credit for. We had several fine conversations during the day's fourteen-mile walk. He volunteered in a refugee center and a homeless shelter/soup kitchen. As we got to know each other we eventually strayed onto the subject of our motivations for making the pilgrimage. Guido admitted to me that he was not sure there was a god, but felt called to do something to make the world a better place. When I told him about my reasons for walking to St. James and asked him to pray for me, he happily and readily agreed. Maybe he was surer about God than he knew.

Joe looks a bit worried as he climbs through the haunted forest toward the Alto de Erro

16. Kendall, *Medieval Pilgrims*, 55.

The day's walk took us through beautiful country, with a few steep climbs and descents. I was grateful that our bodies were holding up well so far. At one point the path looked like the home of the flying monkeys in *The Wizard of Oz*. Dark and overgrown with tangled vines, it gave off a spooky vibe. Once through this wooded section, we summited the *Alto de Erro* and were rewarded with a wonderful view of the rolling countryside.

Several smaller villages dotted the Camino that day. We completed our twenty-two-kilometer day by detouring slightly off the Camino and walking into Zubiri over the *Puente de Rabia* (Rabies Bridge) where it spans the Rio Arga. Some pilgrims continue on at this point and walk an additional 5.7 kilometers to spend the night in Larrasoaña, thus giving themselves a shorter day into Pamplona. We'd had enough, so Zubiri would have to do.

The *Puente de Rabia* got its name from the legend that claims that the mummified body of Santa Quiteria—patron saint of rabies sufferers—was discovered when the fifteenth-century bridge was being built. If farmers lead their animals back and forth across the bridge three times—so the legend goes—the animals will be protected from rabies. Joe and I were only crossing the bridge twice—coming into and leaving from Zubiri. Hopefully we would not come down with anything that caused us to foam at the mouth.

Joe and I secured bunks at one of Zubiri's three pilgrim hostels—Albergue Zaldiko. We shared a room with Lisa and Bart from Maine. They were recently retired from the paper industry and glad of it from what I could tell. We had met quite a few people at our stage of life who were glad to put the rat race behind them.

I logged into the *albergue's* Wi-Fi and retrieved an email from my Aunt Mary Claire telling me that my cousin Francie had gone into hospice care for her lung cancer. My prayers for the rest of the day were focused on Francie and her family.

Joe and I ate dinner at the *taverna* on the corner—an easy five-minute walk from the *albergue*. And yes, Zubiri is small enough that it was not overflowing with intersections. If you instructed someone to "meet at the corner" in five minutes, you could be reasonably assured that she would be there, for there was nowhere else to be. The cafe offered a pilgrim menu of either steak, salad, and fries (my choice) or *paella* and chicken (Joe). We shared a table with two women (imagine Thelma and Louise from the Hollywood movie). They were from California and had visited Lourdes before starting the Camino. Their ecstatic recounting of the Lourdes experience combined with the three—maybe four—glasses of Rioja red wine induced them to generously pick up the tab for our dinners. In exchange, I showed them some tips for how to lace their boots to deal with the blisters they developed that day. This was a pretty good deal for us. The Camino provides, evidently.

Our Zubiri *sello (photo credit: Edmond Kirtz)*

We had a great day on The Way between Roncesvalles and Zubiri. I closed the day with Compline, the evening prayer of the Liturgy of the Hours, which included a short section from St. Paul's Letter to the Ephesians (4:26–27): "*Do not let the sun set on your anger, and do not leave room for the devil.*" Lord, purge me of my anger, and help me to be an agent of reconciliation.

The next day we would walk to Pamplona—our first big city on the Camino. As I fell asleep, Sir Walter Raleigh's seventeenth-century "The Passionate Man's Pilgrimage" played through my head, with its references to quiet, faith, joy, and salvation.[17] A very good way to end a very good day.

Walking Past the Bulls

I awoke at 6:00, surprised to have experienced a decent night of sleep. Well, decent for an *albergue*. Our early morning routine was growing more

17. Raleigh, "Passionate Man's Pilgrimage," https://www.poetryfoundation.org/poems/44940/the-passionate-mans-pilgrimage.

efficient, and we hit the road at 6:45. It was still pitch black, and we hiked for forty-five minutes with headlamps. It rained during the night, but our luck held and it quit in time for us to begin.

The first town we came to—and the place we hoped to find breakfast—was Larrasoaña. We had to leave the Camino and cross the river to access the town. One hundred eighty-three souls supposedly live in this burg, but we walked from one end to the other and did not see a living human being. A few dogs and the odd crowing rooster made themselves known to us, but not a man, woman, or child was to be found. And where there are no people, there is no breakfast. We moved on.

After thirteen kilometers, we took an alternate path so we could visit the church of St. Stephen in Zabaldika. The Camino places these forks in the pilgrim's path from time to time. And each time it does, Joe and I had to have a wee conversation about whether we should go left or right. How tired are we? What additional distance is involved in taking one route or the other? What's to see in this direction or in that? Did the coin flip come up heads or tails? The decision to divert to Zabaldika was a good one. The Belgian Sacred Heart nuns welcomed us warmly, asked about our pilgrimage, and encouraged us. They even let us climb the circular staircase to the top of the bell tower and ring the bell—the oldest bell in Navarre. This pilgrimage must have been having its intended effect on us, for we found that ringing the bell was pretty cool. When one's life is simplified, even the simple things give outsized pleasure.

I took the opportunity at many points along the day's route to offer prayers for a colleague from whom I was separated. My cousin Francie was also very much on my mind. Fun-loving and always the life of the party, Francie and my other Anhut cousins were an important part of my childhood memories. It grieved me to know her illness would eventually end her life. I also offered a prayer for a former student who recently wrote to me to let me know of a serious health concern. The prayers I spoke during the miles and miles of walking were an important part of turning the Camino into a long-form retreat. I was grateful for the time and solitude to be able to focus my heart in this way.

**The Belgian Sisters of the Sacred Heart provided another *sello*
for our pilgrim passports**

Joe and I walked into Pamplona through its eastern suburbs. We had
a good laugh when pilgrims Luis and Maria Claudia asked if we knew the
way. We explained that we were searching for the yellow arrows that mark
the path and they said they had been following us, assuming we knew what
we were doing. We enjoyed their company during the last couple of miles to
the old city. Social workers born in Columbia, but living and working in San
Francisco for the past thirty years, they expressed dismay with the present
state of affairs in the United States. So they had resigned from their jobs,
traveled the world for seven months, and were moving back to Columbia
to try to turn some land they had purchased into a subsistence farm. They
were very engaging people. I was sorry to be losing them as countrymen.

The medieval and the modern in Pamplona (Zarateman/Wikimedia CC0 1.0)

Forty-five minutes after entering Pamplona's urban environs, we crossed the Magdalena Bridge and entered the city's old town through the Old City Gate—the *Portal de Francia*.

Navigating through the big city turned out to be more challenging than simply following the Camino from village to village. Still, we found our way without too much trouble to the Jesus y Maria Albergue near the cathedral. The *albergue* supported a school for developmentally disabled persons, and was housed in the cloisters of a former church (perhaps a sad commentary on the state of the church in Europe). Joe and I seemed to be the oldest *peregrinos* in the *albergue*—by twenty years.

After checking in, we walked to the cathedral square and ate our lunch on a bench surrounded by pigeons and tourists. The cathedral was a beautiful structure stuffed with priceless art. We also wandered about the cloisters and adjacent museum, which had a wonderful exhibit on the development of the West. The cloisters were being set up for a private corporate event. I was sorry to see such a magnificent and historic sacred space used for this purpose. We had been in Pamplona for one hour and had been in two churches, both of which were being used for reasons that would cause their founders to roll over in their graves.

Pamplona Cathedral hosts two munching pilgrims

Pamplona is a college town. Its three major universities enroll more than fifty thousand students. After dinner, Joe and I strolled the Plaza del Castillo and its several side streets. We discovered where all those students spend their evenings. The bars and restaurants were positively overflowing with youth. They spilled out of every doorway and filled the streets. Some stood and talked to friends. Some danced with upheld arms, juggling beers with both hands. Some sat in circles in the street simply enjoying the nearly manic vibe. The next day being Friday, perhaps they planned to take the day off. Those that did attend classes certainly did so with fuzzy heads.

Pamplona is best known for its annual running of the bulls during the festival of San Fermín. Fortunately for us, the festival is in July. During those days the city swells with millions of visitors, most of whom are dressed in the traditional white pants and shirt with bright red sash and neckerchief. These *Ferministas* sleep wherever they can find an unoccupied flat space, though they do not sleep much during this nonstop celebration.

Pamplona and its *Ferministas* (Pixabay)

As we made our way back to the Jesus y Maria Albergue for a night of well-earned rest, I offered a short prayer of thanks for Joe. He was a great walking partner. He was always pleasant, unfailingly kind to everyone he met, and instinctively generous. I could not have asked for a better friend on this journey. This is something not to be taken for granted, as the fifteenth-century pilgrim Felix Fabri understood well: *"For if a man has a comrade with whom he cannot agree, woe betide them both during their pilgrimage!"*[18]

18. Kendall, *Medieval Pilgrims*, 54.

The stamp of the Jesus y Maria Albergue—an outreach of the ASPACE nonprofit

Forgive Us Our Trespasses

The Camino's natural alarm clock—"*albergue* bag rustlers"—awakened me at 6:00. With a gentle nudge, Joe's eyes opened and we took stock of the day's possibilities. Our trip itinerary called for a possible rest day in Pamplona, but after a quick check-in with each other we decided that our legs wanted to walk, so we put on our packs and strode westward out of Pamplona as the sun rose. We skirted the University of Navarra on the edge of the city before moving into open farmland. None of the students we saw the previous night were up and about. No big surprise.

The anxieties that accompanied the preparation for and the first couple of days of the pilgrimage were melting away as Joe and I entered a daily rhythm of wake, pack, walk, pray, eat, walk, walk, walk, find a bed, do laundry, eat, pray, and sleep. The simplicity of the routine dissolved the stress of the unknown. We had also started to gain confidence that the Camino would provide what we needed. Perhaps not always what we wanted, but surely what we needed.

Joe and I paused at 8:30 in the Pamplona suburb of Cizur Menor for a breakfast of *cafe con leche* and Napoleons. Napoleons are basically chocolate-filled croissants, and have the addictive properties of opioids. We had grown very fond of these coffee breaks after an hour or two of walking in the morning. Cizur Menor was a bit depressing, with block after block of drab apartment buildings. If you've heard Pete Seeger's "Little Boxes" you'll get the idea.

Joe and I stopped in Zariquiegui—our guidebook informed us that this village was almost wiped out by bubonic plague in the fourteenth century. This one-horse town is just short of the summit of *Alto de Perdon* (Mount of Pardon). We used the opportunity to take our shoes and socks off to air our feet. We had not been as disciplined as we should be to do this once every couple of hours. This was something for us to work on in the coming days. I visited the thirteenth-century Romanesque *Iglesia de San Andrés* there and offered a prayer for the day's special intention—a renewed friendship with a close colleague from whom I was estranged.

My constant companion on the climb out of Pamplona

On the climb to *Alto de Perdon* we passed a young man pushing a developmentally disabled pilgrim in a wheelchair. It was an amazing sight. The ascent to this windmill-festooned ridge is not that steep, but it is long, and took us able-bodied pilgrims several hours to make the climb. This man's sacrifice on behalf of his wheelchair-bound friend has caused me to check my pride for those occasions when I think I'm serving others. We asked around and learned that this special pilgrimage was sponsored and supported by a Spanish nonprofit—*Camino Sin Límites* (Camino without

Limits).[19] The able-bodied pilgrim was Oliver. He was pushing his brother, Juan Luis, who had a 96 percent disability caused by cerebral palsy. They began the Camino two days after we did, and were committed to walking the entire way to Santiago de Compostela without deviating from the path to take roads.

The high peak of the day was the *Alto de Pardon*. This ridgeline offered 360-degree views back toward Pamplona and southwest toward Puente la Reina and the Rio Agra valley. The mountain is home to forty huge electricity-generating windmills. They looked so small when we started walking toward them as we left Pamplona that morning. Once we were standing directly under them they looked impossibly huge. Another delightful feature of this place was the array of cutout sculptures representing medieval pilgrims making their way to St. James. There is an inscription on one that reads *Donde se cruza el Camino del viento con el de las estrellas* (Where the way of the wind meets the way of the stars). Joe and I lingered awhile at this scenic place and let the cooling breeze dry our perspiration-soaked shirts.

Where the way of the wind meets the way of the stars

The walk down from the *Alto de Perdon* was a treadmill of stones. And it was very steep. And covered with rocks. We were glad to finish that section. We were walking in front of an Italian couple who had a device

19. https://olivertrip.com/Camino-sin-limites/.

playing a beautiful opera—stunningly matched for the rolling hills and pastoral countryside. As the lovely music broke over us, spreading beauty everywhere, Joe broke into the Oscar Meyer Wiener jingle. This proved to be a light moment for the two of us that led to singing jingles and other songs from our youth. These songs were well timed as we were beginning to tire. I doubt the Italians appreciated it. I could not blame them.

Pilgrims sing and play music, and for many reasons. Walking for hours every day can be boring. Singing helps the time pass in a pleasant way. Singing with others builds community. Singing is enjoyable. Singing can be a form of prayer. Indeed, the Catalan people have a saying: *Donde hay musica no puede haber cosa mala* (Where there's music there's no evil).[20] The 427 *Cantigas de Santa María* commissioned by Alfonso X in the thirteenth century were sung by pilgrims to Santiago de Compostela during those days. Jews making the triannual pilgrimage to the temple in Jerusalem sang the Psalms of Ascents (Pss 120–134) as they went up to offer sacrifice. Joe and I would share (and even compose) many songs before we reached Santiago de Compostela, where we looked forward to seeing Maestro Mateo's carvings of the Elders of the Apocalypse playing their instruments in the cathedral's world-famous *Portico de Gloria*.[21]

Music would come to frame the moments of our pilgrimage in strange and wonderful ways. And not just our pilgrimage—indeed, our friendship as well. Even though Joe's ears would bleed a bit as I croaked out fragments of songs to beat back the devil as we climbed, strolled, dragged, shuffled, and otherwise put miles under our feet, the music would be something that I will always remember about the Camino. Br. Simon Teller explained it well when he asserts that music has the power to preach without words.[22]

Near Uterga we stopped to pray at a path-side shrine to the Blessed Virgin Mary. Joe and I consistently observe the near-mania for the Virgin here in Spain. In nearly every church we visited over the course of five hundred miles (many—and perhaps most—were named for her) she occupied the principal place of honor on the amazingly ornate retablos. Jesus on the cross—where he could be found at all—was typically off to the side or positioned so high up near the ceiling that to focus one's gaze upon him was to risk a sprained neck. Indeed, James Michener claims that Mary "has become the central fact of Spanish theology and perhaps of Spanish thought

20. Starkie, *Road to Santiago*, 245.

21. Webb, *Medieval European Pilgrimage*, 156.

22. Teller, "Preaching."

in general."[23] In support of this assertion he describes the last execution carried out by the infamous Spanish Inquisition in 1826. The prisoner was Cayetano Ripoll, a teacher. Accused of heresy for deist ideas acquired while fighting in France, he was strung up for failing to pray the Hail Mary with his students.[24]

Even in a church where Jesus Christ is the only appropriate object of worship,[25] Mary's influence is ever-present. Why is Spain—and The Way of St. James in particular—so "Marycentric"? It may be the case that Mary's image—especially in the form of Madonna and Child, the *Theotokos* (Godbearer)[26]—served as a kind of comforting, soothing counterweight to the potentially frightening morality tales commonly carved on church doors, lintels, pillars, and other ecclesial architecture. These scenes were meant to help form medieval minds and hearts for the divine judgment that awaited them. The fear of hell, with its burning, grotesque demons, and the pleasures of heaven, with its adoring angels, was an ever-present daily reality in the enchanted times in which these churches were built. Perhaps Mary and the promise of her loving, maternal intercession helped to soften the moral weight of life in those times.

Images of the Last Judgment welcome the medieval worshiper at the Bourges Cathedral (Cornell University Library/Wikimedia)

23. Michener, *Iberia*, 728.

24. The more expansive account of Cayetano Ripoll's heresy—and the deism that landed him on the gallows—can be found at Wikipedia, s.v. "Cayetano Ripoll," last modified February 16, 2022, https://en.wikipedia.org/wiki/Cayetano_Ripoll.

25. Charles Freeman has gone so far as to claim that medieval veneration of saints and their relics represented an extension of pre-Judeo-Christian polytheism. Freeman, *Holy Bones*, 29.

26. Freeman, *Holy Bones*, 40.

Devotion to the Virgin has been called the "central fact" of Spanish thought

We decided to hop off the trail around 2:30 in a village called Obaños, which was just a few kilometers from Puente la Reina. We walked about fourteen miles that day. We were pooped, and the more tired we got the more incomprehensible our Spanish became. Eventually we just started calling the place Obamaville. After wandering around this village of eight hundred without locating the *albergue*, a helpful lady took pity on us and walked us around the corner to our home for the night—Albergue USDA. We wandered through a small *tienda* (shop) in Obaños, killing time before the 7:00 Liturgy of the Word at the village church—*Iglesia San Juan Bautista*.

We has observed a number of pilgrims traveling the Camino on bikes. These so-called *bicigrinos* (contrasted to the foot-powered *peregrinos*) have a very tough job. Some of the trails we walked were really tough, and I'd hate to try to ride a bike up or down the steep slopes on the wet, muddy rocks. *Bicigrinos* are considered by some to be second-class pilgrims, but this seems like an unfair judgment based on what I saw. They would earn their *compostelas*. In the Basque Country through which we walked it was common to see—especially in the evening—the local *fronton* as a gathering place for children being tended by their mothers. These courts are used for the Basque game of *pelota*, but it was common for us to see grammar school *matadors* playing at bullfighting.

We ate dinner in a bar where an international array of pilgrims was seated together at a long table. We met a couple about our age from Austria where, like in Germany, the Camino de Santiago is known as *Jakobsweg*. A French woman shared our table. She was an international business executive who was taking some time from her hectic professional life to enjoy a bit of the country in which she engaged in so much commerce. Americans, Brits, and Canadians rounded out the dinner party. It's worth noting that the Camino has been a magnet for international pilgrims for a very, very long time. The royal chancery of the medieval Spanish kingdom of Aragon recorded "safe conduct" letters for the period 1378–1422 for pilgrims from Sicily, Naples, England, Poland, Hungary, Germany, the Flemish region of modern-day Belgium, France, and Tuscany. Pilgrims from Scandinavia were known to travel to St. James—including the Swedish St. Birgitta in 1341. Even Indians and Ethiopians made pilgrimage to Compostela in those days, just as they do today.[27]

Eventually we wandered back to the *albergue* to get ready for bed. My thoughts as I considered the events of the pilgrimage thus far landed on one of Thomas Merton's prayers. Even Merton—the great Trappist theologian and mystic—struggled to "see the road" ahead of him. Like Merton, I hoped that my desire to please God would, if fact, please him. I hoped so, and still do.[28]

Our Obaños *sello*

27. Webb, *Medieval European Pilgrimage*, 144.

28. Merton, *Thoughts in Solitude*, 79.

Pilgrim Bombing in the Nest of Vipers

I woke up refreshed after my best night of sleep yet. I was very grateful for this. By this point in our pilgrimage we awoke rather automatically around 6:00, either because the village church bells ring the hour or because our fellow *peregrinos* begin to stir, rustle bags, cough, and break wind. Joe and I were, of course, perfectly quiet and never disturbed anyone by our movements. And it goes without saying that all of our bodily emanations were discreet, silent, and perfectly agreeable.

We walked in the dark for a little more than two kilometers along narrow dirt paths near the edges of farm fields, eventually arriving in Puente la Reina. This town is where the four principal routes to Santiago de Compostela that originate in France and "points east" come together to form a unified *Camino Frances*—the French Way. Being hungry—we were always hungry—finding breakfast was a priority. A bar at the edge of the town was open, and we tucked into a *cafe con leche* and a *tortilla patata* (a kind of dense crustless potato quiche). I was pleased to be walking in the morning through this ancient town with its historic bridge over the Arga River.[29] I am not sure if Puente la Reina's ancient custom is still in force of ringing the church bells forty times at both nine and ten o'clock in the evening to alert pilgrims walking in the dark that their destination for the evening is nearby.[30] Puente la Reina had a festival that month where competitors raced each other using pitchforks as stilts. I am not sure exactly when the festivities took place, but we were there too early in the day to see much except the roosters disturbing the populace's sleep.

A few minutes after we arrived at the cafe a fellow pilgrim walked in and joined us at our table. Richard—seventy-ish—was a New England native residing in San Francisco. He was a chatterbox, and easily carried the conversation while Joe and I munched and nodded. He felt obliged for some reason to launch into a friendly but vigorous defense of his identity and lifestyle choices. Joe and I listened respectfully, assured him of our gratitude for his companionship on The Way, and told him that we hoped to see him again. Wishing each other *buen Camino*, we took advantage of the bathroom (first rule of the Camino: always take advantage of a bathroom) and took our leave. We would see Richard at several places as we

29. The royal gifts that provided Puente la Reina and similar bridges helped make the Way of St. James the busiest road in Christendom. Freeman, *Holy Bones*, 104.

30. Starkie, *Road to Santiago*, 175.

made our way to Santiago de Compostela. He always walked alone, but was never without a broad smile, a hearty greeting, and willingness to share the news of the road with us.

Puente la Reina (The Queen's Bridge) over the Rio Arga

It was hard to believe that we left Holland only one week before. What a difference in experience and outlook one week can make! I prayed that the pilgrim prayer of St. James would continue to guide and encourage us. That day's prayer intention was for a member of my former administrative team with whom I hoped to be restored to friendship. I received several notes of encouragement from friends wanting to know how we were faring. These notes—along with the daily texts from family—were so comforting. I looked forward to them with great anticipation.

I was not sure if the gray skies on our walk between Obaños and Estella were to blame, but it felt as if a certain "sameness" was beginning to characterize the journey. I knew this was likely to happen, so I was not surprised or discouraged. The routine was helpful in some ways. It allowed for a certain rhythm to our prayer time. It helped with our ability to antici-pate issues with route-finding. And it also helped us in getting to know how our feet and legs would respond to the rigors of the walk.

The route that day was fairly gentle, with mostly flat walking except for a short climb just before Mañeru. The path through the countryside was frequently lined with wild blackberry bushes. Joe was fonder of these than I was. They were too seedy for my tastes. There were many other berry-bearing bushes as well, including the red crap-your-pantsberry. There was also something that looked like a blueberry, but was actually the dreaded Spanish shitberry. We avoided eating those.

We witnessed a funny moment in Cirauqui—in Basque, "nest of vipers"—which is not exactly a chamber of commerce five-star rating of a town name. Cirauqui sits on a hill, and the narrow streets wind sharply and all run uphill. We came into a small plaza containing some apartments, a pharmacy, and a *tienda*. A couple of kids—perhaps ten years old—hid behind the potted plants on their third-floor balcony. While one prepared the camera to capture the moment, the other tossed firecrackers from the balcony to startle pilgrims as they came unawares into the plaza. And startle them they did! This was amusing enough, but the real show started when an old man in the plaza started yelling at the kids—presumably chastising them for their rowdy behavior. Well, grandma, who was watching the kids, came storming out of the apartment and began laying into this fellow and the brouhaha was on. I did not understand the words exchanged between the two of them, but my sense of the conversation was something like this:

> **Old Man**: Hey! You good-for-nothing brats, cut that out or I'll tell your parents!
>
> **Grandma**: You leave them alone, you old codger. I'm their grand-ma and I'll do the disciplining around here!
>
> **Old Man**: Well, what are you waiting for? Those urchins of yours are bombing the pilgrims!
>
> **Grandma**: Don't tell me how to manage children, you shriveled waste of skin. Go manage your own grandkids and leave mine alone!

Etc., etc., etc., at length and loudly. When the old man was suitably chastised by Grandma, he wandered over to us as we munched on a snack on a nearby bench. He began speaking to us in Spanish spoken too quickly for me to absorb, but I can imagine that he was fomenting on the state of dissolute youth these days. Joe and I nodded sympathetically, mumbling, "*Si, si, es la verdad . . .*" until he had vented his spleen and wandered off.

This fellow met his match from Grandma on the balcony

I walked the section between Lorca and Estella with a young woman, Jane from Wilmington, North Carolina. She had graduated from college four years before, worked for a while, quit her job to go to work in her parents' business, and quit that too. She seemed like such a nice person—an able conversation partner and all-around lovely young lady. She was trying to discern her future while walking the Camino. We spent quite a while discussing her vocational confusion. She seemed a bit lost at that stage of her life, which saddened me. Our conversation made me feel like a college professor again, and it felt good. I sure hope Jane's Camino provided the clarity she was seeking.

My conversation with Jane led me to wonder how safe single women feel tramping the road to Santiago. The electronic pilgrim forums have many conversation threads on this subject. Though there have been instances of violent crime on the Camino, these seem to be relatively rare. Whether this has more to do with the shared sense of *communitas*, the economic incentive that Spain has in keeping the way appealing for tourism, or the general virtue of the Spanish people, I could not say. Perhaps it is a legacy of the ancient protections afforded to pilgrims from French and Spanish kings—and even from popes. At the Lateran Council of 1123 Pope Calixtus

II ordered that anyone who robbed a pilgrim would be excommunicated.[31] Harsh, perhaps, but in those days, I imagine it was an effective deterrent.

The author of the first pilgrim's guide to the Camino, Aymeric Picaud, has much to say in the twelfth-century *Codex Calixtinus* about the various peoples and rivers one encounters along the way. He is particularly harsh in his judgments about both in the first Spanish stages:

> *The horses die at Rio Salada. At a place called Lorca, to the east, flows the river known as the Salt Stream. Be careful not to drink it or water your horse there, because the river is lethal. On its banks, as we were going to Santiago, we found two Navarrese sitting there, sharpening their knives, waiting to skin the horses of pilgrims which die after drinking the water. When we asked, they lied and said the water was safe to drink. So we watered our horses, and two died at once, which the men then skinned.*[32]

The first pilgrim guide to the Camino de Santiago, the twelfth-century *Codex Calixtinus* (manuel m. v./Wikimedia (CC BY 2.0)

We were grateful to see no skinned horses or scheming Navarrese bandits lying in wait as we walked over the Rio Salada in Lorca. In fact, Lorca seemed like a pleasant little village. As proof, the skies cleared and brightened to a brilliant blue. It seemed we had avoided the rain again. Our guardian angels deserved a raise.

I coined a new term that day. "Pre-tired" is what one feels before moving into a state of abject fatigue. The fifteen miles we walked moved me from "pre-tired" to "pretty darn tired" at about mile fourteen. It felt good

31. Mullins, *Pilgrimage to Santiago*, 71.

32. The English Version of book V (Codex Calixtinus).

to check into the *albergue* in Estella, which was a converted school and doubled as a youth hostel. Even though we were tired, I was glad we were walking. Early English and Irish pilgrims to Santiago de Compostela made the first part of the trip by ship. The trip was often difficult, as the anonymous poem from the time of Henry VI in the fifteenth century attests:

> *Men may leve alle gamys*
> *That saylen to Seynt Jamys*
> *(You leave behind all fun and games*
> *When you set sail for Saint James)*[33]

We attended the Saturday vigil Mass at twelfth-century *Iglesia de San Pedro de la Rúa*. The church possessed several relics, including a piece of the True Cross and Saint Andrew's shoulder bone. It was a church of fantastic beauty. We received a pilgrim's blessing following the Mass, which was very meaningful to us both.

The long walk up the steep hill to *Iglesia de San Pedro de la Rúa*
(Zarateman, CC BY-SA 3.0 ES, via Wikimedia Commons)

The relic known as the True Cross has an interesting history in Catholic tradition. There are various accounts of how the cross upon which Jesus sacrificed his life for our sins was discovered, but they generally agree that Empress Helena, the devout mother of Emperor Constantine, found

---

33. Anonymous, "Pilgrims' Sea Voyage."

the cross during a pilgrimage to the Holy Land in 326–328. Bits of wood alleged to be remnants of the cross have multiplied to the point that they can be found in churches all over the world. John Calvin, an obvious skeptic of the True Cross tradition, had this to say about the dispersal of relics from Helena's discovery:

> *There is no abbey so poor as not to have a specimen . . . if all the pieces that could be found were collected together, they would make a big ship-load. Yet the Gospel testifies that a single man was able to carry it.*[34]

There is a rather large fragment of the True Cross in the Monastery of Santo Toribio de Liébana located on the Camino Norte—the northern route to Santiago de Compostela that runs along the Bay of Biscay through the Cantabrian Mountains. Pilgrims routinely stop at the monastery during their journey to St. James to pray before this relic. The True Cross has had a powerful impact on the Christian imagination outside of the medieval West. The monk Nestor of Kiev (1056–1114) claims that Vladimir I drove the devil out of then-pagan Russia through the power of the True Cross.[35] The True Cross even had a role to play during the Allied invasion of Normandy during World War II. Some of the fifteen thousand denizens of Caen huddled in the convent of Notre Dame de Bon Secours during the terrible bombing intended to drive the German army from this important city. Mother Superior led them out through the chaos holding a relic of the True Cross before the shell-shocked procession.[36]

Belly Up to the Bar

When I arrived in Spain, I could not sleep. I then transitioned to the point where I slept better, but woke up very early without prompting. But in Estella it took the alarm feature on my phone to wake me up at 6:00. Progress! All outside was dark and damp. Our beds were comfortable and bade us linger awhile. But Mr. Frost's reminder that "we've miles to go before we sleep" spurred us. Up and at 'em.

The Albergue Juvenil Ocineda that served as our Estella accommodation was a youth hostel, though there were pilgrims staying there too. It

34. Carter, "Why We Can Have Faith."

35. Cross and Sherbowitz-Wetzor, *Russian Primary Chronicle*, 149.

36. Beevor, *D-Day*, 268.

was a pretty nice place, except when hordes of teenagers returned to the building long after we had gone to bed. They made an unholy racket late into the night. It would have been a great youth hostel with fewer youth. There was also a troupe of Napoleonic war reenactors sharing the hostel with us. When they were not out in the fields around Estella drilling, charging, retreating, and feigning death, they were in the Albergue Juvenil Ocineda whooping it up like regular soldiers on leave. They were certainly enjoying themselves. Still, seeing inebriated accountants and lawyers dressed up as if it was Halloween while stumbling down the halls carrying swords and other deadly things gave us pause.

Stamp of the Albergue Juvenil Ocineda in Estella

That morning my right foot hurt near the head of the second metatarsal. I took naproxen and hoped it would be OK. I was not sure if I stepped too hard on a rock (or a billion rocks) or if the pain was caused by the cumulative miles starting to impact the spare parts God used to create my feet. I hoped this would turn out to be a manageable, business-as-usual ache and nothing more.

The day's prayer intention was for a fellow professor. I hoped we would be able to reconcile. Joe and I prayed a rosary as we walked between Villamayor de Monjardin and Los Arcos. I dedicated it to renewed friendship with those from whom I was separated, to family and friends who were sick, and to friends who had been such a faithful presence in my life, including and especially my wonderful family.

One of the things that pilgrims to St. James look forward to is stopping by the Bodegas Irache. Why? Because this place had a fountain that dispenses a delicious local red wine. For free. To anyone. Regrettably for us and the other pilgrims with whom we are walking, the spigot was not turned on. I guess that 8:00 on a Sunday morning was too early to imbibe on the fruit of the vine—even for Spaniards. In any case, this was a very cool thing to see. There was an inscription near the fountain:

> *Peregrino! Si quieres llegar a Santiago con fuerza y vitalidad de este gran vino echa un trago y brinda por la Felicidad (Pilgrim! If you wish to arrive at Santiago full of strength and vitality, have a drink of this great wine and make a toast to happiness).*

Fill 'er up at the Irache wine fountain. Note the carving of *Santiago Peregrino*.

Every day we walked we saw something that amazed us. Often we saw many things that amazed us. Sometimes they were things that we would not have noticed if we were in a car and traveling at speed. The slow pace of foot travel made for keen vision, which ultimately allowed for a deeper level of discernment. The day's "amazing thing"? We saw a guy running the Camino. With a backpack. Five hundred miles. As if that was not enough of a challenge, he was also singing. At the top of his lungs. Amazing.

The Camino has had since medieval times purposes that extend beyond the purely religious or even vaguely spiritual. It has also been a kind of economic engine that, it must be said, has kept many small villages alive. We walked through places nearly every day that seemed moribund except for the *taverna, tienda,* and *albergue* that encouraged pilgrims to spend the night and leave a few euros behind. The Camino also attracts entrepreneurially minded musicians, artists, and vendors selling everything from pilgrim souvenirs to light snacks. These folks pop up in the most unlikely places. We were walking along through seemingly uninhabited precincts on that day when—all of a sudden—we heard the faintest shadow of a soulful melody coming from someplace. We walked along the dirt path for a few more minutes, winding our way through groves of trees and past enormous haystacks, when suddenly—in the literal middle of nowhere—we spied a man and woman playing the violin and accordion to the great delight of passing pilgrims. It was lovely.

An unlikely but delightful musical interlude on the path between Estella and Los Arcos

I'd been mentally doodling the outlines of a poem as we walked over the previous couple of days:[37]

> *Dusty roads, take me to Compostela.*
> *City streets, take me to Compostela.*
> *Forest trails, take me to Compostela.*
> *Country lanes, take me to Compostela.*
> *Rocky paths, take me to Compostela.*
> *Gravel tracks, take me to Compostela.*
> *Muddy traces, take me to Compostela.*
>
> *Steepest hills, take me to Compostela.*

37. "Take Me to Compostela: A Poem," https://www.youtube.com/watch?v=Bi1SdAVOBk4.

Gentle slopes, take me to Compostela.
Painful descents, take me to Compostela.
All flat places, take me to Compostela.

Ridgeline windmills, take me to Compostela.
Soaring cathedrals, take me to Compostela.
Ancient chapels, take me to Compostela.
Haunted ruins, take me to Compostela.
Bustling cities, take me to Compostela.
Sleeping villages, take me to Compostela.
Crossroad shrines, take me to Compostela.

Blistered feet, take me to Compostela.
Darkening toenails, take me to Compostela.
Quivering muscles, take me to Compostela.
Aching knees, take me to Compostela.
Groaning back, take me to Compostela.
Hunched shoulders, take me to Compostela.
Sun-kissed neck, take me to Compostela.

Wind and rain, take me to Compostela.
Warming sun, take me to Compostela.
Blue skies, take me to Compostela.
Grayest clouds, take me to Compostela.
Moon and stars, take me to Compostela.
Morning mists, take me to Compostela.
Shimmering heat, take me to Compostela.

Endless wheat fields, take me to Compostela.
Mountain heights, take me to Compostela.
Fecund vineyards, take me to Compostela.
Verdant forests, take me to Compostela.
Giant haystacks, take me to Compostela.
Wayside blackberries, take me to Compostela.
Ageless chestnuts, take me to Compostela.

Peregrinos of every nation, take me to Compostela.
Friends at home, take me to Compostela.
Heart-branded family, take me to Compostela.
God the Father, take me to Compostela.
God the Son, take me to Compostela.
God the Holy Spirit, take me to Compostela.
Blessed Virgin Mary, take me to Compostela.

St. James, take me to Compostela.
Communion of saints, take me to Compostela.
Great cloud of witnesses, take me to Compostela.

Take me to Compostela, and refresh my soul.

I have mentioned several of the people we met who were sharing the pilgrimage with us. We seemed to run into these folks from time to time. We might see them in one place and then see them in another village four days later. It was like we were a big community spread out over the miles that came together and split apart, only to come together later. Yakkety-Yak John from the Valcarlos *albergue* seemed to keep popping up. He was always cheerful, and his powers of speech had, if anything, grown even more volcanic since we met on the first day of our pilgrimage.

We walked past many of these on the Camino
(Bob Jones / Giant haystack via Wikimedia Commons)

Our target for the day was Los Arcos—a walk of about fourteen miles. We arrived around 1:30. The day was nice and our energy was sufficient, so we decided to "crack on"—as the Brits say. Had we stayed we might have seen one of the most ornate altarpieces in all of Spain in the *Iglesia de Santa María de los Arcos*. But "Hurry-Up Rich" convinced "Let's-Take-a-Look Joe" that there was nothing to see in this one-horse town and we moved on. This was a mistake, for the church in Los Arcos is really something to behold. I hoped this instinct to get there would teach me a lesson and impart the gift of going slower and seeing more. Joe really did deserve a better partner than me.

As we walked past Los Arcos for the seven-kilometer stroll to Sansol we passed a cemetery with a sobering inscription:

I once was what you are. You will be what I am.

Well. That focuses the mind. As we walked on in reflective silence through the massive vineyard to the west of Los Arcos we came upon an elderly nun making her way slowly—very slowly—along the Camino. She was praying the rosary as she shuffled painfully down the track on swollen ankles that looked like fleshy fence posts. We offered a respectful *buen Camino* to which she responded in kind. Within five minutes we had walked far enough in front of her to lose sight of her. Unlike other pilgrims that are traveling in our "bubble," we never saw her again. This woman was an inspiration to us both. While we may have had our minor daily struggles with being hungry, tired, hot, cold, or sore, this pilgrim—like Oliver and Juan Luis from the *Alto de Perdon*—was a living embodiment of the true pilgrim spirit.

Joe: Should we take a look? Me: Nah, let's skip it. (luisgar/Wikimedia CC BY-SA 3.0 ES)

We walked another three miles to Sansol—population ten—Spain's version of Mayberry. We found the town's *albergue* and settled in for the evening. The *albergue* offered a pilgrim meal for eight euros that we thought was a good idea, this being Sunday in the smallest town in Europe.

While nursing beers at one of the *albergue's* picnic tables we chatted with Arturo, a graduate student from Los Angeles. He was a slightly built fellow weighing perhaps 120 pounds dripping wet. He limped into the *albergue* carrying a huge pack complete with laptop and textbooks. I had seen pilgrims carrying many things that qualified as bad ideas, but Arturo's excess weight won the blue ribbon. The result of this heavy pack weight when added to the long distances he was walking left him with badly blistered feet and a knee that was killing him. He wanted to complete the Camino in only two weeks so he could return home to care for his father following a planned surgery. One simply cannot walk five hundred miles in two weeks unless in possession of superhuman physical gifts. I gave him some naproxen, encouraged him to lighten his pack, and asked him to consider taking a bus ahead to Sarria so he could arrive in Santiago de Compostela within the limited time he had available.

João from Brazil joined our table for dinner. He was a *bicigrino*, biking to Santiago de Compostela. What an affable and agreeable dinner companion! An attorney with his nation's federal justice ministry, the airline lost his bike and luggage. Undeterred, he simply started walking, which he did for three days until his equipment was located and forwarded to him. I learned an important lesson from João. Stay flexible and keep moving forward by any means necessary.

I'd intentionally avoided adding up the miles we'd walked or how far there was to go. Why? It felt too early in the pilgrimage to begin to look toward the end. Mile-counting would, I thought, put me in that frame of mind. Enjoy the moment. Enjoy the day. That was my motto.

Our Sansol *sello*

Adios Navarre

It was a chilly night in the Albergue Deshojando. I slept well, but needed leggings, my sleeping bag liner, and a blanket for warmth. Like many men "of a certain age," I occasionally need to get up in the night to answer nature's call. Doing so in the well-traveled halls of my cozy home is one thing, but navigating the pitch black from the upper bunk of a strange hostel involves certain hazards, including (a) falling off the bunk bed, (b) rattling the bed—which always squeaked like the rusty hinges on Dracula's coffin lid at the slightest movement, (c) tripping over backpacks, boots, hiking poles, and other impedimenta, and (d) getting lost in the dark on the way to wherever the hell the bathroom is. Our evening in Sansol was such a night. After I groped my way back through the dark after my potty break, I noticed that my phone had lit up with a message. My daughter-in-law, Lindsey, had sent photos of my granddaughters, Norah and Greta. My heart filled, I fell easily and happily back to sleep to await the 6:00 alarm.

Joe and I packed up in the dark. I was getting better at being able to do this by feel alone. Clothes went into one stuff sack. Gear went into a second. Both went into the backpack. Finished. I peeked outside and was gratified to see the first moon and stars of the trip. Perhaps we would be blessed with clear skies for pilgriming that day. We hoped so.

In less than a kilometer we came to the village of Torres Del Rio (Towers of the River) with its two churches—*Santo Sepulcro* and *San Andres*. It was too early to see much of the town, so we passed directly through. Just west of Torres we came to a place in the forest where pilgrims had left prayers and reflections written in many languages on slips of paper tucked into rock cairns. Many hundreds of pilgrims had planted these prayers in this sacred place. We lingered for thirty minutes reading them. They were impactful testimonies to the power of prayer contained in those notes. Here are two examples:

> *Please pray for Deidre who is battling breast cancer. Stay strong Deidre.*

> *Since I am no more than a dot in this world and all the shit that was thrown in my face by life and by my own doing. I can leave a piece of my addictions here in this place. Going cold turkey on the Camino has been the best decision ever. Walk hard. You're the only one who can.*

A small fraction of the hundreds of prayers left by pilgrims

The Camino was largely uninhabited, with few towns between Sansol and our ultimate destination of Lograño. The stretch between Torres Del Rio and Viana was nearly eleven kilometers of dirt paths, farm fields, and a wetland that hosted migrating birds in season. Though the track was fairly flat, our legs warmed a bit as we climbed the *Alto el Poyo* with its small *Capilla de la Virgen del Poyo*.

Eventually we reached Viana. Viana was a reasonably large town by Camino standards, with over four thousand residents. One of the town's principal landmarks is the spectacular *Iglesia de Santa Maria de la Asunción*, which serves as the burial place of Cesare Borgia, son of the infamously corrupt Pope Alexander VI (1431–1503). Joe and I prayed Lauds in front of the church's fantastic high altar.

The Camino enters most towns from the east side, is directed down the main street, and exits on the west side, spitting pilgrims back out into the countryside. This route placement has strengths and weaknesses. On the one hand, the Camino often directs pilgrims past the principal shops, restaurants, cafes, bars, and points of interest. But there are often hidden treasures that can be found if one is willing to deviate from the route and poke around a bit. We did some of this, but not enough. We were more likely to explore off the route if the town was bigger, we were staying the night, and our *albergue* was a tad off the beaten path. In places like Viana we often did not linger beyond a coffee break and peeking into the church. I would do it differently next time.

Waymarking on pilgrimage routes is a very old phenomenon. Pope Damasus (d. 384) had scripture verses inscribed on catacomb walls in Rome[38] to guide pilgrims wishing to visit the burial places of the earliest Christians.[39] Maps were not the only way we made our way from here to there along the Camino. The route was marked in frequent intervals by a combination of yellow arrows (*flechas amarillas*), granite waymarkers (*mojóns*), scallop shell symbols, and other forms of signage. Some of the markers were commercially produced and reflected attention to standardization common to the road signs we see in everyday life. Some of the markers were simply spray painted on any available flat-ish surface— a rock, wall, post, or sidewalk. And some markers were delightfully and creatively composed homemade works of art that provide enjoyment to pilgrims as they strolled by. While the Camino was generally well signposted, this aspect of the experience did have its ironies. Sometimes the straightest country lane—the one with absolutely no deviations to the right or to the left—was marked by *mojóns* on both sides of the path every one hundred yards. Only the world's most confused bumbler could lose the way in these places. But in other locales—often in larger cities where the roads diverge in many directions with lots of other signs and visual distractions— the *flechas* were practically invisible. We had to pay close attention to keep to the way—especially when leaving a city in the inky darkness of morning. We spent very little time each day actively thinking about the route. We learned to glance around when the path crossed a road, at intersections, and other times when we had choices to go right, left, or straight. The correct choice was usually obvious. On those few occasions when we stood at an intersection with confused looks it was common to hear a whistle from up the street. We would look in that direction and spot a local Good Samaritan pointing us in the right direction. The Camino provides.

---

38. Pilgrims to Rome were called roamers. The verb "to roam" is derived from the pilgrimage tradition to Rome.

39. Kendall, *Medieval Pilgrims*, 41.

Not sure which way to go? Just point your shadow to the west.

As we entered Logroño we said goodbye to Navarre and hello to La Rioja. It felt good to have walked through an entire region! The walk up into Lograño was a bit gritty and industrial, but we were cheered by a light-hearted conversation with Neil, a Scotsman living in London. Logroño is the capital of La Rioja—a region best known for its vineyards and wine production. A city of over 150,000 people, Logroño offered us the chance to see more than what was offered by the typical Camino villages through which we typically walked. Some pilgrims did their best to avoid these larger cities, feeling that they lack a sense of the Camino spirit that smaller towns exemplify in such abundance. If I ever return to the Camino I may adopt this practice. There is a drawback, however. Larger cities provide a nice opportunity to take an occasional rest day. Being stuck in a flyspeck on the map—while restful and quiet—is pretty boring. Burgos and León offered a host of interesting and diverting sights. Sansol, on the other hand, would have provided little except the opportunity to watch the grass grow— if it was not already crisped to straw by the Deathstar that is the summer Spanish sun. With this in mind, we considered pushing through Logroño and on to Navarrete, but we were leg-weary enough that the extra eight miles didn't seem desirable, so we checked into the municipal *albergue*.

Hello Lograño

Logroño was hosting its annual Fiesta de San Mateo, a wine festival featuring grape crushing exhibitions. Joe was looking forward to a glass of Rioja red. The sixteenth-century physician and Compostela pilgrim Andrew Boorde offered advice that Joe and many other modern-day pilgrims had no trouble following:

> *Pilgrims should have a good strong drink of wine at the end of their long day's tramping, before going to bed. "If they be Englishmen,"* *he adds, "ale should be their drink, for ale is a natural drink for an* *Englishman, even as beer is a natural drink for a Dutchman. As to* *wine, it doth actuate and doth quicken a man's wits, it doth comfort* *the heart, it doth scour the liver."*[40]

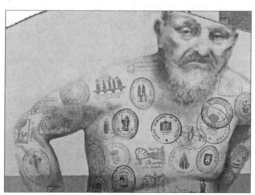

Logroño graffiti

40. Starkie, *Road to Santiago*, 6.

The day's landscape was pleasing indeed. Gently rolling hills, forested trails, and some terrific long views made for light hearts and strong legs. And it was a blue-sky day, with cool temperatures that made hiking a pleasure. Still, we were glad to cross the graceful bridge over the Rio Ebro and arrive at our destination. Logroño provided many delightful memories, including a series of parades in honor of San Mateo. While lounging around the Calle Laurel with its many eating and drinking establishments we enjoyed watching the late afternoon social habits of the native Logroñans. Workaday folks were dressed in their best clothes as they strolled the boulevard—sometimes referred to as *la senda de los elefantes* (the elephant walk)[41]—enjoying a pre-dinner coffee or *apéritif*. The *Plaza del Mercado* adjacent to the cathedral was filled with people strolling from one activity to the other, including mock bullfighting activities for kids. Magicians, clowns, and stages being set up for a concert were on offer. There was a lighthearted, fun vibe in the atmosphere.

After dinner we wandered back to the *albergue* to retire for the evening. The building seems like it might have been a multilevel school in an earlier age. Our bunks were on the third floor in a room that accommodated perhaps three dozen pilgrims. The atmosphere was a bit institutional—even sterile—but it was home for the night. Grateful for a good day, I offered thanks for the day's many blessings, prayed for forgiveness of my many sins, inserted my earplugs, and drifted off to sleep.

The stamp of the Riojana Friends of the Camino in Logroño

41. Drink enough Rioja wine and you may begin to walk on all fours while weaving from side to side—like an elephant.

And They Shall Know Us by Our Limping

Albergues are a bit like restaurants. Sometimes a restaurant looks so inviting, with an appealing menu, charming decor, and plenty of curbside appeal. When the meal arrives, however, the food is bland and cold. Other restaurants have the atmosphere of an establishment where automobiles are serviced, but the food is to die for. Joe and I experienced *albergues* that did not look like much but had a wonderful, all-in-the-family culture that made everyone smile no matter how road-weary they were. The Logroño municipal *albergue* was not one of these. It was crowded and stuffy. Though it had a nice patio and kitchen, the sleeping rooms felt like a prison. Our room had a single window that needed to be left open for ventilation, but gave access to the 4:00 a.m. catfight taking place down on the street. There was a bad snorer a couple of rows away from me. "Bad snorer" is a kindness of the most generous sort, actually. The sound coming from this guy was otherworldly, like something straight out of the *Blair Witch Project*. One of the Italian guys finally got out of bed and poked him, which caused this epiglottisly challenged pilgrim to roll over and settle a bit. I was glad for my earplugs, which helped, but not enough.

We left Logroño in the dark, but by this point in my story you know that we always left in the dark. The sanitation workers were trying to clean up the trash in the streets from the big all-night fiesta, which was a real rager if the geologic strata of empty beer bottles were any indication. There were still roaming bands of dissolute youth haunting the streets at 6:45, but they gave us a wide berth. No doubt we intimidated them with our pointy hiking poles and all-around rugged pilgrimness. Rugged pilgrimarity?

We had an eighteen-mile day, so we breakfasted while we walked, which consisted of fruit and crackers we purchased the night before. After wading through the beer bottles and growling our way past the pimply inebriates, the walk out of Logroño proved very pleasant. The route took us for miles through the beautiful *Parque de la Grajera*, with its lake, forest groves, thoughtfully placed benches, and picnic tables just waiting to be occupied by families enjoying a weekend outing. Lovely.

Seven hours of walking requires creativity to keep a conversation going. Sometimes things get silly, like when Joe sang through the catalogue of the St. Pat's School songbook. On that day we made a list of things we hadn't seen in Spain:

- Hot air balloons
- Chipmunks
- Pepper on the dinner table
- Window screens

Of all the things on this list, the item most urgently desired was window screens. And this is evidently a very old problem. Aymeric Picaud in his twelfth-century *Guide du Pèlerin* (Pilgrim's Guide) warns pilgrims bound for Santiago de Compostela to cover their faces while traveling through the French region of Bordeaux because of the peskiness of the flies that reside there.[42] The flies, while not carnivorous or particularly aggressive, were abundant enough to merit a complete refit of every Spanish window frame. They did not exactly blot out the sun, nor could anyone claim that they were one of Pharaoh's plagues. That said, we spent lots of time brushing and swiping both in and out of doors. I like a bit of pepper in my food. Chipmunks are delightfully diverting as they frolic playfully about. Who does not enjoy a hot air balloon framed by a perfect blue sky? But give me a window screen.

After about twelve kilometers we came to the small town of Navarrete. Upwards of two thousand people allegedly lived in this town, though where they were, I could not say. The streets were quiet. Perhaps San Mateo was honored here as well and people were still sleeping, recovering from a night of wine-soaked revelry. Our guidebook alerted us to the fact that the church contains one of the most excellent *retablos* in all of Spain. In fairness, the guidebook often gushes forth about some aspect or another of the zillion churches in this tunnel of Christendom through which we had been walking. In the case of *Iglesia de La Asunción*, the guidebook was as understated as a mud fence. The altar in this church was beyond description. To call it ornate is to do it an injustice. It was a soaring monument in gold. My eyes did not know where to look first. An entire day spent sitting in its presence examining it square foot by square foot would be insufficient to fully appreciate its many wonders. If this church was located in the United States it would be a national treasure. In Spain it is just another dying parish in a backwater village.

---

42. Kendall, *Medieval Pilgrims*, 43.

Iglesia de La Asunción, **Navarrete**

My feet were growing sore, so I was grateful for the moderate grades and forgiving footpaths we experienced that day. And naproxen. I had never been more aware of the simultaneous inadequacy and durability of my feet until the Camino entered my life. For the most part, my feet had just been the body parts to which I had attached shoes every morning for sixty years. I had been able to make my way through each day more or less oblivious to their presence. The Camino focused my mind in a much more attentive way to my feet. I came to esteem them with a heightened centrality among all the various bones, organs, and sinews from which I am constructed. Each day as I tramped the Camino's paths, sidewalks, and cobbles I found myself in conversation with my feet in new and fresh ways. "We're hot and sweaty. Stop soon and air us out or we'll make trouble for you. We mean business this time." I learned to take orders from my feet, who I now recognize as the captains of the ship that sailed me from France to the Atlantic.

These socks are "guaranteed for life," but maybe not life as a pilgrim

Most of the day's walk was through agricultural areas—primarily wine grapes, but also some wheat. Indeed, most of the Camino traverses this kind of geography. A long walk is a wonderful thing in part because it helps one appreciate the blessings of variety. Just as our minds began to tire of endless vistas filled with abundant vineyards—lovely as they were—an interesting village would appear on the horizon. Suddenly the surrounding landscape—a fit for an artist's brush—seemed less captivating as our minds leapt forward to what was next. "I wonder what's in that village? What does our guidebook say about it? Come to think of it, I'm a bit hungry. I wonder if it has a cafe. A coffee would be nice. That is an interesting bell tower on the church. I wonder what the interior is like? And a bathroom would be very welcome as well." We walked through the town with its interesting diversions (or lack thereof) and were spit back into rough countryside. Rinse and repeat.

I was glad we did not have to sleep here

My aversion to mile-counting became impossible in La Rioja. The good people who mark the way there had thoughtfully included the distance to our ultimate destination on many of their signposts. From that point forward it was difficult to avoid counting miles, my best intentions notwithstanding. The guidebook said we had 363 of the original five hundred miles left to go. We were getting there.

After we passed through Ventosa we came to the spot where—according to legend—Charlemagne's brave lieutenant, Roland (he who met a grisly end at Roncesvalles, courtesy of Basque steel), dueled gallantly against the Saracen giant Ferragut. The giant was huge. Grisly of countenance and iron-limbed, with single-handed skill and superhuman force he defeated dozens of Charlemagne's finest champions, killing them outright or sending them to dank Muslim prisons. Finally, Roland—nephew of the emperor—stepped forward. The battle—*mano a mano*—lasted three days. This being a civilized fight to the death, breaks were evidently allowed for *siestas* and restful evening slumbers. The antagonists even found time for engaging conversation on such wide-ranging topics as the Holy Trinity, the book of Genesis, the Immaculate Conception of Mary, and the resurrection of Jesus.[43] During one of these palavers, Ferragut—evidently being stronger than smarter—let it slip to Roland that his only weakness was a soft spot near his navel. Being a practical fellow, Roland used this intelligence to his advantage, slipping his spear into the giant's breadbasket, saving the day for Christianity.

We got beds in Nájera's Albergue La Juderia-Sancho III, which is a strange name that I still can't quite figure out. The *refugio* was decidedly common, and nothing fancy for our ten euros. We did not find out that it lacked Wi-Fi until after we'd paid our money. During the first days of the pilgrimage this would have bothered me, but I was learning to roll with minor inconveniences, and starting to appreciate that all inconveniences are minor in the grand scheme of things.

Albergue La Juderia-Sancho III. Hmmmm . . . La Juderia? La Juderia refers to the Jewish section of a city—what today we understand to be a ghetto. Perhaps Nájera once had a thriving Jewish quarter. Perhaps it still does. In any case, Jews have a complicated history in Spain. Some historians believe that Phoenician trading routes brought Jews to Spain as early as the Old Testament times.[44] There is little question that at one time Jews were both abundant and well off in Spain—making it one of the largest population centers of Jews anywhere in the world. But in 1492 the Catholic king and queen, Ferdinand and Isabella—who brought us Christopher Columbus, the Spanish Inquisition, and other creative ways to decrease the surplus population—issued the Alhambra Decree, forcing so-called *Sephardim* to either convert to Catholicism or leave the country. A quarter million Jews are estimated to have converted, with perhaps one hundred

---

43. Gerritsen and van Melle, *Dictionary of Medieval Heroes*, 71.

44. Hinojosa Montalvo, *Los Judíos en la España Medieval.*

thousand choosing exile. Today there are no more than fifty thousand Jews remaining in Spain.

It felt good to take a shower, clean our clothes, and rest after a long day of walking. Joe shared a room with Erin from Maine (who we met in Sansol) and Andy from near Cologne, Germany. I bunked with Blaise and Claude, the Frenchmen with whom we shared a room in Zubiri. They were nice guys, but spoke no English. Since I speak no French beyond a few polite words, we shared a lot of hand gestures and Google Translate.

As I lay in my bunk reviewing the pilgrimage and its lessons, the day's Gospel from Luke was on my mind:

> *Then his mother and his brothers came to him but were unable to join him because of the crowd. He was told, "Your mother and your brothers are standing outside and they wish to see you." He said to them in reply, "My mother and my brothers are those who hear the word of God and act on it." (Luke 8:19–21)*

I hoped I was hearing His word and acting on it. I hoped.

The stamp of Albergue La Juderia-Sancho III in Nájera

Holy Chickens

As Joe and I walked, biked, lifted weights, swam, and climbed from April to the end of August we wondered if we would ever actually step onto the Camino. Now that we had progressed this far, I found it hard to believe that we would leave the Camino for hearth and home, kith and kin in one month. What would the month bring?

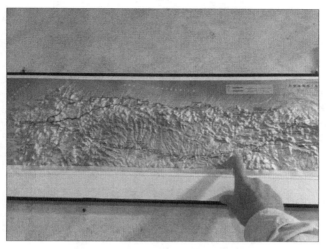

Walk from here across the rest of Spain in a month? ¡Si, Se Puede!

The Frenchmen and I bumped into each other as we packed up in the cramped space of our shared bunk room. We were good natured about it with plenty of *excusez-moi* and *merci*, but I think we were all glad to escape each other's intimate gravity. I had a feeling these fellows were going to be part of our pilgrim bubble for quite a while as our pace seemed pretty evenly matched.

Leaving town in the dark with our headlamps lighting the way was by now a comfortable habit. We were especially careful to scan for *flechas* along the path in the dark. Under those circumstances it was best to pretend we were driving in a Michigan snowstorm, hoping the car in front of us knew where the road was. This principle seemed to work just as well for pilgriming.

A brisk five-mile walk took us to our breakfast in Azofra. *Cafe con leche, tortilla patata,* and *pan* (bread) was tasty fuel for a twenty-eight-kilometer day. Our guidebook did not have much to say about Azofra and its 250 inhabitants other than to note its presence along the Camino. *TripAdvisor* informed us that Azofra had a botanical garden. The nine people who visited found it commendable. We passed.

The most interesting thing about Azofra presented itself 1.5 kilometers west of town. There we encountered a fifteenth-century *columna de justicia*—a stone boundary marker. Exactly what boundary it was marking had, apparently, been lost to the mists of history. In any case, I stood next to it, with my left foot in someplace and my right foot in someplace else. Camino excitement at its most thrilling.

This boundary marker used to be important. To someone. We think.

The Camino provided the nicest day for walking yet, with cool temperatures moderated by the warming sun and brilliant blue sky. This was surely the day that the Lord made. Joe and I rejoiced in it, and were glad.

We were getting better about stopping to rest, removing our shoes and socks, and airing our feet. As we donned dry socks during these rest stops, we pinned the damp ones to the outside of our packs, where the sun baked them dry in no time at all. All this footwear changing made us feel like souped-up Indy cars changing tires every fifty laps. Near Cirueña we stopped for a tire change and bought some fruit from an unemployed path-side vendor. As we did so we heard the rapid-fire *patois* of Claude the Frenchman rounding the corner. Claude and his walking buddy, Blaise, had been our shadows for some time. They always had a hearty "*Ça va?*" for us. They were completely aware that neither Joe nor I spoke any French whatsoever, but Claude chattered away to us as if we hung on his every word. We nodded and smiled.

We had planned to spend the night in Santo Domingo de la Calzada. We pulled into town around 12:30, found a bar, and had lunch. It felt too early to quit, and our legs felt strong, so we decided to push on to the next town—Grañon.

First, though, we thought we would take a look inside the grand cathedral that houses the holy chickens. Both Chicago's Wrigley Field and the nation of India may have holy cows, but Santo Domingo de la Calzada, way out on the sun-kissed plains of northern Spain, has holy chickens. These blessed foul, provided all that any chicken could ever want as they clucked contentedly in their gilded coop high up on the cathedral wall, are said to be the direct descendants of the chickens that were miraculously resurrected so very long ago. A pious family of pilgrims to St. James—mother, father, and son—were passing through Santo Domingo when weariness overcame them and they stopped for the night. The daughter of the local family with whom they lodged took a shine to the young man. When he spurned her lusty advances, she secreted a precious object in his traveling sack and reported him as a thief to the magistrate, who promptly strung him up in a scene reminiscent of the rough justice of the nineteenth-century American West. The boy's parents—shattered by the loss of their only son—naturally continued their pilgrimage. Here accounts vary, but one way or another they discovered—either on their return trip or in a vision—that their son was, improbably, alive. When they rushed to the magistrate's home to report the fantastic news and reclaim their boy—obviously innocent as evidenced by the fact of his continuing sentience—he told them that their son was as dead as the roasted chicken presently occupying his dinner plate. The chickens stood up and crowed lustily. That's the miracle. And that's why Santo Domingo de la Calzada has chickens in its cathedral.[45]

---

45. Walter Starkie claims that the miracle was "a godsend" to the town, as interest in the pilgrimage to St. James along the "old road" from Nájera to Burgos had diminished in the fourteenth century. He speculates the legend was part of a propaganda campaign by local innkeepers to attract pilgrim business. He goes on to describe a "parlor trick" mentioned in an ancient Italian pamphlet that fools the observer into thinking a roasted chicken has been brought back to life: "Take a drop of brandy, a chip of celery and a crumb of bread and soak the crumb well in brandy. Then put the chip of celery on the soaked breadcrumb and feed it to the chicken and it will immediately fall to the ground as though dead. Then you must pluck the fowl and smear it all over with honey and saffron, which will give it the appearance of having been roasted. When you wish the fowl to jump at table, all you have to do is moisten its beak with strong vinegar and straightaway the bird will stand up in the dish, as has been proved." Starkie, *Road to Santiago*, 208–9.

The "holy chickens" of the cathedral at Santo Domingo de la Calzada
(PMRMaeyaert/Wikimedia CC BY-SA 4.0)

We felt pressed for time and did not want to pay three euros to tour the museum just so we could see the church. Or the chickens. We got our pilgrim passports stamped and hightailed it out of town.

The stamp of the Cathedral of Santo Domingo de la Calzada—holy chickens included

The character of the landscape was beginning to change. We were entering a land with few trees and little shade. Unending miles of rolling fields of harvested grain swept to the horizon like waves on the sea. It was pretty in its own special way, though I suspected we would be glad for the forests of Galicia when the Camino took us there.

Shepherds tending their flocks near Santo Domingo de la Calzada

Nearly every day we came across something that qualified as a head-scratcher. Two places that day qualified for this distinction. Joe and I were walking along a dirt farm road seemingly miles and miles from anything. Blue sky and brown fields were all we could see. And what did we spy off to the left? Lawn furniture. For pilgrims. Made of concrete. Whoever placed these conveniences here for our use was mighty thoughtful. Mighty thoughtful indeed.

The second thing that had us wondering was the village of Cirueña. The guidebook described it as a ghost town with a population of 131. The number of ghosts is unspecified. Cirueña's *Wikipedia* page contains two sentences. The construction of the buildings was modern. And in a world-turned-upside-down sort of way there was a nice golf course at the entrance to the town. It seems that the tough economy rendered this development ill-timed.

Grañon was a sleepy little place to which we arrived around 2:15 after walking through a hot afternoon with miles of rolling wheat fields. We checked into the *Albergue Casa de las Sonrisas* (House of Smiles), claimed our beds, showered, and "laundered" our clothes. If you have ever opened up an issue of *National Geographic* and seen photos of third-world women slapping their wet clothes on flat rocks in the village stream then you'll have some idea of what our laundering habits were like. Being a persnickety engineer, Joe was a bit more diligent than I. He located the *albergue's* washtub, lathered his sweaty togs lavishly, rubbed the grimy spots with plenty of elbow grease, rinsed everything thoroughly, and hung his shiny-clean hiking uniform in a sunny spot for the fresh Spanish breeze to dry for use the following day. I simply wore my clothes into the shower, removed them there, stomped on them a bit as I scraped the road off my body, gave them a good squeeze to get most of the water out, threw them on the line, and hoped I did not forget about them if it started to drizzle. Once dry, Joe carefully folded each article and painstakingly placed it into its own plastic bag, which was then inserted into just the right place in his well-organized backpack. My mostly dry clothes, on the other hand, were simply stuffed into a stuff sack. I mean, it's called a *stuff sack* for a reason. Joe smelled no better than I did, so you decide which was the better method.

Joe and I attended the daily Mass in Grañon's *Iglesia de San Juan Bautista*. As with other Masses along the Camino, pilgrims were called to the altar for a special blessing at the end of the Mass. Though this was spoken in Spanish, the priest's sincerity and obvious warm wishes for us *peregrinos* shone through and offered great encouragement.

Pilgrim-themed window in *Iglesia San Juan Bautista* in Grañon

Ernesto, the *albergue's hospitalero*, prepared a meal for the pilgrims. There were twenty of us crammed around a table designed for ten, and it was a lot of fun. We were the only Americans, with lots of Italians, the always-present Frenchmen, a couple of Catalans, two Germans, and a Brazilian. The food was delicious. The goodwill freely shared around the table was even better.

Our Grañon stamp with its scallop shell

Owen

As lovely as the dinner the previous evening was, the breakfast offered by the Grañon *albergue* was quite awful. Instant coffee warmed in a microwave oven was paired with something akin to what the Brits would call a "digestive." There were crusty loaves on the table, but they look suspiciously like the crusty loaves that we saw when we arrived the day before. They looked a bit mouse-nibbled. And they had the tensile strength of iron bars. We stuck with the "coffee and digestives" section of the menu. Not that there was a menu. I put twenty euros in the donation box to cover my bed, dinner, and the five-star breakfast. I felt I had done my duty under the circumstances.

A short time after we left the darkened streets of Grañon we walked out of La Rioja and into the third region of our pilgrimage—Castilla y León. We would walk through this province for four hundred long kilometers until we hit the last section in Galicia in far northwest Spain.

Half of the Camino would be in this autonomous state

We stopped for coffee and Napoleons in Redecilla del Camino after only four kilometers. We were joined by plenty of other pilgrims seeking the same thing. Our "second breakfast" consumed, a potty stop before hitting the trail was in order. A common feature of bathroom lights in Spanish *albergues* and bars is that timers control them, and they will automatically shut off after about one minute. The first time this happened I scrambled around feeling for the light switch in the pitch dark from the, uh, seated position. I learned my lesson—eventually—and came to scout the position of the light switch before I, well, you know . . . So much to think about when one is a pilgrim.

The walk that day was long and largely shadeless. Much of the route ran close to the busy N-120 expressway—a major east-west thoroughfare through northern Spain. We covered seventeen miles from Grañon to Villafranca Montes de Oca. There was little to capture the imagination or divert our attention from putting one foot in front of the other. A technique that I learned to rely on when there was not much of interest to see was to ask Joe a question of a technical nature. His electrical engineering experience in the automotive industry provided a deep well from which to draw. And Joe was both generous in his responses to my inane questions and patient when I sought clarification. I asked him what he thought would be different in automobiles ten years in the future. "Well, let me tell you . . ." That conversation took two hours. Joe was a great way to pass the time. I hope he got something from me out of our pilgrim partnership. I sure am better for his presence.

High-end Camino graffiti in Belorado

The afternoon grew warm, so I broke out my umbrella and rigged it to my pack to provide some shade. I drew looks and not a few comments from some of the pilgrims we encountered. I cannot tell if they thought I was being clever or ridiculous.

The view from under the shade umbrella during a long, hot walk

We were twenty-three miles from Burgos, a large city where we hoped to get a hotel for two nights to rest and recover. Part of me wanted to push hard to get to Burgos the next day. But we were already a day and a half ahead of schedule, and I did not know if it was worth it to push so hard. My right calf was sore and I wanted to avoid injury if possible.

We picked an *albergue* in Villafranca Montes de Oca that was associated with a luxury hotel. I wondered if the hotel had a hard time making a go of it during the recession and decided to try to get some productive use out of part of the property. In any case, the place was pretty nice for an *albergue*, offered a twelve-euro pilgrim meal in the restaurant, and was located well away from the busy road that ran through town past the municipal *albergue*. We chose well.

We went through our normal *albergue*-arrival routine. Check in. Get our *credencials* stamped. Claim a bed. Take a shower. Wash clothes. Relax. The ever-present Frenchmen joined us shortly and were as cheerful and friendly as always.

One day after completing my daily stair climbing in preparation for the Camino, I saw an elderly couple in the parking lot slowly shuffling toward the stairs that snake up the dune. It was a hot, humid day. I was positively lathered with perspiration. As I stood next to the car toweling off and trying to stop sweating, the octogenarians made their way over for a chat. She looked a bit like Strega Nona, with wispy gray hair flying to all compass points. He had oversized wraparound sunglasses perched awkwardly on his nose. "Are those walking sticks?" asked Priscilla as she pointed toward my high-tech hiking poles. "Yes, they are," I responded. "They really help me on those steep stairs." I asked if they were planning to climb the stairs. "Well," said Priscilla—clearly the pair's official spokesperson, "we climb the first twenty-five stairs, rest awhile, then come down backwards. It's easier on our old knees." All the while, her manfriend, Owen, was eyeballing my car—a no-news grey Ford Fusion. "I used to work for the company that manufac-tured your automobile," Owen croaked. Strega Nona elbowed him in his substantial midriff and instructed him in a no-nonsense manner to tell me what he did at Ford back in the day. For a moment I wondered if he was old enough to have worked with Old Henry himself. After Owen recovered his wind he asked me if I'd ever heard of the Ford Gran Torino. "Sure. That's a famous car," I replied. "I designed it," he responded, much to my astonish-ment. At this Priscilla wound up and whopped him again in the gut. "Tell him what else you designed," she barked. Owen—now a bit pale from the combination of his verbal exertions and his ladyfriend's pugilism—asked me a second question. "You know those double-necked guitars that some rock 'n' rollers play? I designed those too. For Elvis Presley in 1959. That V-shaped guitar is also one of my designs." You could have knocked me over with a feather with this intelligence. I felt I was standing in the pres-ence of creative genius. We palavered for a while longer before they tottered off for their afternoon constitutional.

At dinner I chatted with a South African pilgrim who, in a rather offhand way, mentioned that another fellow at the end of the table was from Nashville and "did something in the music business." After dinner I strolled down to his end of the room and introduced myself, interested to know more about his Nashville work. He told me he was a guitar designer. I told him the story of the day in July when I met Strega Nona and You Know Who. "Was his name Owen?" my new pilgrim friend inquired.

Sometimes the Camino seems like a five-hundred-mile magic trick.

The pilgrimage is a rich opportunity for prayer, and I was doing my best to use the vast empty spaces and long miles to focus on the intentions that occasioned the pilgrimage in the first place. Joe and I prayed the Rosary daily—usually during the last hour of the walk. I have the best family anyone could ever hope for, and they were always the object of my gratitude during my prayers. I also prayed for genuine and authentic reconciliation with those at the college from whom I was separated. I'd have to be patient to see how this might bear fruit. The spiritual weight I carried with me to Spain was starting to feel a bit lighter.

The *sello* of the Hotel San Antón Abad in Villafranca Montes de Oca

Los Caidos

The path leading westward from Villafranca Montes de Oca tilts steeply up into the Forest of Oca, where the early morning mists swirled around us like ghosts in the inky darkness. Walking in a forest one knows well gets one's imagination going. Walking through strange country in the dark had a certain "Hound of the Baskervilles" effect on my mind. While Joe and I never felt at risk of brigands or highwaymen while pilgrims on the Camino, *peregrini* in earlier times were frequently in harm's way. Kings and popes both did what they could to ensure pilgrims' free and unmolested passage, including prohibiting taxes and tolls. A truce between the sovereigns of France and England in 1440 included a provision for free passage of pilgrims between the two countries.[46] Still, pilgrimages in those days remained dangerous, which is one reason *peregrini* made their wills and settled all their affairs before departing. Hopefully the thousand pilgrims

46. Webb, *Medieval European Pilgrimage*, 39.

killed in the twelfth-century fire in Vézelay[47]—one of the principal French starting points for the Way of St. James—had taken such precautions.[48]

How far you have to go depends on where you're heading

Within a short while after leaving the *albergue* we came to a monument marking the burial place of three hundred people killed during the Spanish Civil War. *El Monumento de los Caídos* (Monument to the Fallen) honors those who supported Franco in that terrible war. It has a kind of stark simplicity that was haunting when illuminated only by the headlamps of pilgrims. All wars are awful, of course, and the Spanish Civil War was no exception. Death estimates vary widely, but historians grimly agree that there were atrocities aplenty.

47. Vézelay is the traditional location of the relics of St. Mary Magdalen. Cartwright, *Catholic Shrines*, 84–87.

48. Kendall, *Medieval Pilgrims*, 51.

A grim reminder of the war's impact in the Forest of Oca
(KRLS/Wikimedia CC BY-SA 4.0)

As the skies began to lighten, we came upon Jackie and Terry, a retired school psychologist and secretary from California. This was their second Camino, and they were delightful. We would see them here and there all through the day, and eventually end up at the *albergue* in Cardeñuela de Riopico together. We also spent time walking with Emily and Andreas, whom we had met a few days earlier and had encountered in various places since then. They were hiking together rather exclusively. Sparkin'?

We stopped for a refreshing snack and a coffee in Agés, population sixty-five. The cafe was delightfully festooned in scallop shells, flowers potted in discarded pilgrim boots, and other Camino-themed items. The mist of the early morning had burned off, and skies were a deep, satisfying blue.

We walked through Atapuerca later that day. Archeologists assert that the earliest human remains in Europe were found there. *Homo antecessor* lived sometime between 1.2 million and 800,000 years ago. The remains of this cannibalistic human predecessor were discovered in 1994, and an archeological park was established to help educate the public about this branch of the human family tree. Joe and I were anxious to get to Burgos— and our first rest day—so we skipped the tour and pushed past the town without pausing.

Speaking of Burgos, I cannot say with precision why I wanted to get to this city so badly, but I felt the pull of it very strongly. Perhaps it was because a rest day sounded lovely right about then. So did a bed—a bed without an attached ladder—with a pillow of exquisite softness that would envelope my head, neck, and shoulders like an infant in his mother's lap. The room would have a door. A door that locked. And the room would have a toilet and a shower that I would be more than happy to share with Joe. Nobody else would use it. And it would have towels, real towels—delightfully fluffy, made of the purest white cotton, and luxuriously large. Not at all like the battleship grey chamois that was stuffed into the dark recesses of my pack. The chamois that was no larger than a piece of paper. And the only other sounds of human functioning that would be heard in this room would be Joe's occasional emanations. I would not have to listen to farting in six languages. No plastic bags would rustle. No alarm would awaken me. And when I strolled the tree-lined boulevards of the city I would do so unencumbered by a pack and without the need for hiking poles. Yes, Burgos would be like an island of civility and refinement in this never-ending pilgrim stream. Get me to Burgos.

There's not always something to see on the Camino, but sometimes . . .

We got our first view of Burgos after summiting the very steep, rocky path leading to the Matagrande Plain. The area off to our left as we climbed was a restricted military area from which we could hear ordinance being fired over the hills. Did I mention that I was anxious to get to Burgos? Well,

I developed my first blister while powering up the hill to the Matagrande Plain. Ugh. I worked awfully hard over the summer to toughen my feet in the hope of avoiding that very problem. And we had seen some horror movie blisters on pilgrims since coming over the mountains. These were blisters of biblically leprous proportions. I had to be more careful. I felt the slightest zing of discomfort on the side of my left big toe, and when I arrived at the *albergue* and removed my socks, there it was. Drained and dressed, I hoped that was that.

Burgos was just too far for us to make it all the way on that day, so we pulled in at the Albergue Via Minera in Cardeñuela de Riopico before the temperature heated up too badly. It grew pretty hot later, which made for pesky flies. All in all we were glad to get off the road and get off our feet. Burgos and its many charms would wait one more day. We would have a walk of just over seven miles to reach downtown of Burgos in the morning. It seemed strange to think that we would at that point be about 40 percent of the way to Santiago de Compostela.

All the *hospitaleros* seemed to work very hard to meet the needs of the *peregrinos*, and the guys at Albergue Via Minera were no exception. They positively flew around the community dining room in the hour before the dinner to get ready for the full house that would partake of their hospitality. And the dinner they prepared was an affair both lively and enjoyable. We sat next to Anders and Simone from Munich. They began their pilgrimage in Passau in Bavaria and had already walked three thousand kilometers over seventy-three days, which seemed incredible. They shared many tales of pilgrim derring-do with the group, including having to bus through Switzerland because of the terrifically high costs of food and lodging in that country. They also mentioned being rescued in a torrential French rainstorm—in the dark—by a guardian angel who drove them to a monastery where they were sheltered from the elements for the night. The next morning, the anonymous trail angel showed up at the monastery and drove them back to the point where they were forced off the Camino. It should be noted here that Anders seemed much more animated about their harrowing experiences and near-death moments than did Simone, who mostly nibbled glumly as Anders prattled on. If I was forced to hazard a guess, I would say that Simone longed for the comforts of Passau, and Santiago be damned.

The group of young Italians who were part of the pilgrim wave we'd been traveling in (and who were part of the animated pilgrim dinner in

Grañon) rolled into the *albergue* around 4:00, accompanied by lots of rapid-fire chatter. I had a hard time discerning whether they were arguing or just engaged in normal conversation. There was lots of arm waving, words with sharp edges, and finger pointing—all followed by laughter and knowing nods. I guess everything was OK, but sometimes I scratched my head in confusion once they wound up. They were a blast again at dinner at Albergue Via Minera. One of them started singing and before long they had most of the room clapping along, yelling *bravos*, and calling for *encores*.

After dinner Joe and I chatted with Bernard, a pilgrim from a small town near Montreal. In 2012 he walked the Camino from LePuy, France, to St. Jean Pied-de-Port—five hundred miles. He was back on the Camino walking the French Way from St. Jean Pied-de-Port to Santiago de Compostela with his godson/nephew. He seemed to be a very nice guy. His nephew sounded somewhat troubled, and Bernard seemed very wise, discerning, and patient with him. He was a good example for me when I returned to working daily with students. His patience with his young charge reminded me of a truth from my pre-administration teaching days: If a professor hangs in there long enough with just about any student, the chances that the student will succeed are high. I was grateful to Bernard for reminding me of this.

My kids have been wonderfully supportive of my pilgrimage. They sent me photos and videos of the grandchildren nearly every day. I was not only grateful for these, they often impacted me emotionally. More than once a tear found its way onto my pillow as I looked at these before falling asleep.

I began praying for a long list of friends, grateful for their faithful presence in my life. We too infrequently thank our friends for the freely given gift of their fellowship and tolerance of our eccentricities. I wanted my friends to know that I appreciated them. I also continued to pray to let go of any lingering anger stemming from my professional downfall. I read *Thoughts Matter*, by Mary Margaret Funk, while on this pilgrimage.[49] Her thinking—which channels the ancient ideas of John Cassian[50]—encour-

---

49. Funk, *Thoughts Matter*, 81.

50. John Cassian was a fourth-century desert father and Christian monk-theologian celebrated in both the Western and Eastern Churches for his mystical writings. Cassian is noted for his role in bringing the ideas and practices of Christian monasticism to the early medieval West. His advice on anger was helpful to me on my pilgrimage. Cassian, *Conferences*, 552.

aged me to root anger out of my soul. Every vestige had to be eliminated. All of it.

In medieval times pilgrimages were commonly undertaken as part of a vow.[51] My desire to be cleansed of my anger was, I suppose, a kind of vow to do the internal work necessary to be worthy of this gift. Medieval pilgrims' vows were serious business, and were often made in public and blessed by the local priest or bishop. My vow was serious too, though if I stumbled for some reason in being faithful to it, I would not have to apply directly to the pope for dispensation or commutation as medieval pilgrims had to do.[52]

As I approached the end of the first third of the pilgrimage, I found myself grateful for this extended opportunity to pray for an end to anger. The fourth-century words of St. Ephraim the Syrian admonish me:[53]

> *This is the first commandment: that you should love the Lord your God with all your heart and soul, and with your strength as much as you are able.*

> *The sign that you love God is this: that you love your neighbor. If you hate your neighbor, your hatred is really for God.*

> *Christ, as he hung on the height of the tree, interceded for his murderers. But you, who are dust, born of the clay—rage fills you whenever you like! You keep anger against your brother, and yet you dare to pray? Even the person standing right beside you, though he is not neighbor to your sins, the stain of your sin reaches out to him, and his petition is not heard.*

> *It is blasphemy if you pray to God while you are angry. For your heart also convicts you that you multiply words in vain. Your conscience rightly judges that your prayers do you no good.*

> *Leave off anger and then pray. Unless you would provoke further, restrain your anger, and then supplicate . . .*

---

51. See, for example, the vow made by the mythical pilgrim Ogygius: "My wife's mother had bound herself by a vow that if her daughter gave birth to a boy and he lived, I would promptly pay my respects to St. James and thank him in person." Erasmus, *Colloquies*, 623.

52. Webb, *Medieval European Pilgrimage*, 56.

53. Socks, "Church Fathers."

Our last stamp before a day off in Burgos, at Cardeñuela de Riopico

El Campeador Welcomes Us

Luxury is ultimately a state of mind. Under the straitened circumstances of the pilgrimage one might consider a 7:00 wake-up *sans* alarm a luxury. I would, and in fact, do. We could walk seven miles to Burgos before coffee, so a few extra winks were welcome indeed. Most of the other pilgrims seemed to have the same idea. No bag-rustlers at zero dark thirty that morning.

Before we left the *albergue* Joe asked me to take a look at a fellow pilgrim's ankle injury. Yuka was a young Japanese woman walking thirty-kilometer days. She developed problems early in her pilgrimage with her left knee, which was much better by that point. Unfortunately, she had been overloading her right leg, and developed a nasty tendinitis in her right ankle. I advised her on some stretching, and encouraged her to take a couple of days off to let it calm down. I hoped she would be OK. If she tried to push through her injury, I have little doubt that it would end her pilgrimage.

Even the humblest householder cheerfully directed us on our way

It was cold and foggy leaving Cardeñuela de Riopico, but the day warmed nicely and bright sunshine cheered us as we walked to Burgos. As we strolled through Orbaneja Riopico we turned a corner and were mildly surprised to run headlong into a *Tyrannosaurus Rex* giving us the eyeball. I guess if you are the mayor of a village of two hundred people, you'll do just about anything to keep folks from driving by on their way to the Big City.

Orbaneja's *T. Rex*

Our route took us past the Burgos airport fence. The airport was blanketed in thick fog, and we neither saw nor heard an airplane. The guidebook described four optional routes into the heart of the city. We decided to follow the route that meanders along the Arlanzón River. Though it was not waymarked all the way into the city, we just kept the river on our right and eventually it led us right downtown.

In 1960 a Moorish roofing tile was discovered just to the north of Burgos. On its reverse side was the text of an epic poem. Which raises a question: Why would medieval authors adorn roof tiles with their poetic musings? Anyway, dedicated to the first Count of Castile, Fernán González, the poem recounted his various heroisms in keeping Castile largely out of Moorish hands during their long Spanish sojourn. He must have been quite a guy. The poet—a thirteenth-century monk of the San Pedro de Arlanza monastery—opened with an impressive gush:[54]

54. Wikipedia, s.v. "Poema de Fernán González," last modified July 18, 2021, https://en.wikipedia.org/wiki/Poema_de_Fern%C3%A1n_Gonz%C3%A1lez.

En el nombre del Padre
que fizo toda cosa,
el que quiso nasçer
de la Virgen preçiossa,
del Spiritu Santo que es
ygual de la espossa,
del conde de Castilla quiero
façer vna prossa.

(In the name of the Father
who made everything,
[of] he who wished to be born
of the precious Virgin,
[and] of the Holy Ghost who is
equal those already mentioned,
about the count of Castile I wish
to make prosody.)

And so on, lavishly, for many pages in Old Spanish, which, thankfully, I cannot read.

As his legendary status grew, various honors were accorded him, including the naming of assorted streets and the moniker of the hotel into which we checked. It was lovely. We showered, washed and hung clothes, took a short nap and headed out to tour the cathedral. Being in a hotel felt like such a luxury. No bunk beds. Only one person to share the bathroom. Actual towels. Pure decadence!

Suitably refreshed, scrubbed, and dandied for our tour of this city of 175,000, Joe and I crossed the street from the Hotel Fernán González, crossed the river by way of the Puente de Santa María, and entered the city's main plaza by way of the Arco de Santa María—a sixteenth-century gate that contains sculptures of various worthies, including our beloved Fernán González. The main event in the plaza is the cathedral, named for . . . Santa María, of course.

Mere words are too thin—too shallow—to do justice to the fantastic nature of Burgos Cathedral. Poetry might work better than prose, I suppose, but in any case, the place was too expansive, too ornate, too Gothic-on-steroids for the inadequacies of language. I have been in many churches in Europe. Most could be described as modest chapels compared to *Santa Iglesia Catedral Basílica Metropolitana de Santa María de Burgos*— a UNESCO World Heritage site.

Burgos Cathedral framed against a blue sky

Joe and I got our *credencials* stamped at the cathedral, where we would attend Mass the next morning. We rented audio guides and spent a couple of hours strolling through the cathedral's many chapels, ambulatory, and cloisters. One of Spain's national heroes is buried under the cathedral's floor. Rodrigo Díaz de Vivar—*El Cid* to the Moors and *El Campeador* to the Christians—is in some ways an unlikely fellow to be so immortalized. Finding his grave so ennobled would be like finding Benedict Arnold buried in the US Capital. He was a dandy in the court of the Christian king of Castile, Ferdinand the Great, and his son Sancho II. He won many battles on their behalf, defeating the Moors through a combination of brilliant strategy and bravery on the field. He also bloodied the noses of Sancho's brothers, Alfonso VI of León and García II of Galicia. When Sancho was assassinated, Rodrigo found himself in a bit of a pickle. Exiled by the new Christian king, El Cid simply switched sides and went to work winning battles for the Moorish ruler of Zaragoza. Eventually a different group of Moors proved such a threat to Alfonso that he begged Rodrigo to come back and work for the home team. After several additional machinations, El Cid decided that he was ready to be his own boss, so he besieged Valencia and eventually created his own autonomous kingdom in that city and the surrounding region.[55] While not establishing a sterling reputation for loyalty, El Cid was enough of a tiger on the battlefield that the burghers of Burgos decided he should be buried in their cathedral with all forgiven. I guess everybody likes a winner.

Where should we look first? (JoJan/Wikimedia CC BY 4.0)

Our time in the cathedral left us with an appetite. We were hungry most of the time. When we found ourselves in the Camino's one-horse towns, the bars, restaurants, and *albergues* tended to make dinner available to pilgrims around 6:00. But when in the big cities, we ate when Spaniards typically eat—late. We wandered over to a string of eating and drinking establishments situated near the river and settled in with a beer and some *tapas*. I tried a black pudding thing and crostini with Serrano ham and tomato. They were good—good enough that I could have eaten several more. And several more after that. To leave room for our eventual dinner, we strolled around until we found a grocery store, where we picked up various victuals for the next day's breakfast and lunch.

55. Fletcher, *Quest for El Cid*, 4.

My blister puffed up again on the walk into Burgos. I re-drained and re-dressed it and hoped that it would heal before I needed to put in some real miles on when we skedaddled from Burgos.

I received some great pictures of my son Matt, daughter-in-law Allison, and grandchild Kennedy as we dragged back to the Fernán González. These were a grand way to end a very good day.

The Burgos Cathedral stamped our *credencial*

Slumming

We enjoyed a wonderful day off from walking the Camino. It was a pleasure to sleep soundly through the night, with no snoring or bag rustling to disrupt our rest. We awoke around 7:30 and lounged around for awhile before showering (another hotel luxury—a morning shower with a real towel), dressing in our "clean" clothes, and heading to Mass at the Chapel of St. Tecla in the Burgos Cathedral. I was especially pleased to be in Burgos on a Sunday. When we had attended Mass in the villages and towns through which we'd passed, the worshippers were few and far advanced in age. Except for our fellow pilgrims seeking the Lord's blessing on their pilgrimage, the churches only seemed to attract the League of the Halt and the Lame. The Church in Spain seemed a bit moribund.

The Chapel of St. Tecla was by no means the largest or most ornate in the cathedral, but it was still fantastic in the extreme. Unlike other liturgies we experienced, this one was well attended, but by very few young people. There was a terrific choir that provided the music for the Mass.

Their quality combined with the acoustics of the soaring ceilings made for a lovely worship experience.

We ran into Carli from New Hampshire at Mass and invited her to join us for coffee and croissants on the esplanade. Carli was in the same *albergue* as us in Cardeñuela de Riopico. Her feet were hurting. She claimed they were getting much better, but she still seemed to limp. She was in between jobs, the last of her sons had just moved away to college, she was divorced, and she seemed like she was hurting a bit emotionally. She was chatty, and tended to carry the conversation, but my instincts told me she was not as whole as she wished to be. Well, who is? I offered a prayer that whatever it was she needed, God would provide.

While enjoying our coffee Thea from Barcelona greeted us. She had been part of our pilgrim bubble and we ran into her from time to time. She told us (in her native Catalan language, which I managed to understand with just a bit of sign language) that her knee and shin pain was sending her home early. After a while two women—one Canadian and one German— greeted Carli to let her know that they too were going home because of blisters and other physical problems. What a disappointment this must have been for them. It made me reconsider my grumpiness over my lone, minor blister.

The charming riverside Burgos *esplanade* was very pleasant on a Sunday morning
(LBM1948/Wikimedia CC BY-SA 4.0)

Our coffee consumed and conversations concluded, Carli and our other friends wandered off in various directions. Joe and I went looking for a *farmacia* where I could restock my dwindling supply of Band-Aids. Before too long we rounded a corner and spotted the familiar green cross. The pharmacist was very helpful in providing me with a wide range of appealing options for Band-Aids in assorted sizes, shapes, and degrees of flexibility. Unfortunately, the antibiotic ointment I was also hoping to purchase was only available by prescription in Spain. I haven't the faintest idea why this simple product—impossible to abuse or even misuse—should be regulated in this way. Fortunately, I had a little left, and could always bum some from other pilgrims if needed. In a pinch I could use alcohol-based hand sanitizer from my toilet kit, but godalmighty did it sting.

Joe headed back to the hotel to use the Wi-Fi while I found a bench thoughtfully spotted in a shady spot on the *esplanade* to journal, read, and people-watch. It was a glorious morning, with many people out enjoying a stroll through the gardens, plazas, and pedestrian-friendly walkways. A string quartet played delightfully somewhere off to my left while the city's churches rang their bells, adding to the beauty of the setting. I watched as a ten-kilometer race came down the *esplanade*, with the serious runners out in front and families—some with young children—bringing up the rear. My prayers that morning were in thanksgiving for the long friendship I've enjoyed with Mike Seymour. Has anyone ever had a truer or more devoted friend than Mike? I am lucky for his faithful presence in my life, and can only hope that I have enriched his life in some small way, for he has surely been a blessing to me.

Idiots abroad

A Sunday afternoon is a very pleasant time for a nap. This is difficult to do when pilgriming, because one is usually out on the road, grinding out the miles to the next destination. But Burgos offered me a respite from such exertions. Thank you very much, Hotel Fernán González, for providing me the chance for a delightful "pants-off, under-the-covers" nap. Wonderful.

Joe and I were tourists for the afternoon and walked around the remains of Burgos Castle, which dominated the heights of the city. It was well worth the two hours it required. This castle was also an *alcázar*, which is a Spanish synonym of Arabic origin, reflecting the Moorish influences of the times in which most of these fortifications were constructed. Still, not all castles—or *castillos*—are *alcázars*. I was flummoxed as to the difference. This castle/*castillo*/*alcázar* was ancient in origin, with some parts dating from Roman times, others Visigothic,[56] and still others medieval. Napoleon's army blew it up as they skedaddled out of town, though the ruins served as emplacements for anti-aircraft batteries during the Spanish Civil War. The views of the city with the imposing spires of the cathedral were rather spectacular.

In the morning we would begin the long walk across the Spanish *meseta* with a twenty-mile hike to Hontanas. It made me a bit nervous—shocking, I know—given that my toe was far from perfect. Many pilgrims take a bus from Burgos to León, skipping the *meseta* altogether. The guidebooks and pilgrim websites spoke of the *meseta* in hushed tones. Landscapes that stretch to an infinite horizon, little shade, a sun that burns with the intensity of a thousand supernovas, choking dust, and scant water were to be expected. One imagined vultures circling overhead for the ten days the crossing required just waiting for a pilgrim to drop, first to one knee, then to hands and knees, and finally face down—never to rise again. I weighed more than Joe, so I do not think it was unreasonable to suppose that the vultures might take a keener interest in me, leaving Joe for other, less discriminating grassland scavengers. I could only hope they would do me the courtesy of waiting until I was truly and irreversibly dead before they began picking at my *meseta*-depleted husk of a body. God save us both. Not wishing to shortchange the vultures, Joe and I found a wonderful little

---

56. The Dark Ages saw waves of invaders break over Europe, through Spain, and all the way to North Africa. One of the last of these barbarian hordes were the Visigoths, who carved out a settlement in Northeast Spain they called *Gothalandia*. Time has softened the name to what we know today as Catalonia—the home of Barcelona. Cartwright, *Catholic Shrines*, 116.

bistro serving a largely pilgrim crowd. We enjoyed a delightful final meal together.

After praying Compline, I was positively tickled to see that I had received a couple of emails from backpacking buddies Joe Dault and Mike Seymour, along with texts from Carol and the kids. Oh, how I loved these lifelines to home. I would call home for the first time later that evening and was really looking forward to it.

Cleopas the disciple as a pilgrim at Emmaus[57]
(Mattia Stom/Wikimedia Public Domain)

---

57. Matthias Stom, *The Supper at Emmaus* (ca. 1633–1639).

The Middle

Meseta Meanderings

THE alarm jarred us out of our dream-filled slumber at 6:00 sharp. Time to get back into pilgrim mode again. We had saved a few items from yesterday's grocery store shopping trip for our breakfast this morning. Packs packed and laces laced we strolled away from Hotel Fernán González at 6:40 and made our way across and eventually out of a still-sleeping Burgos. It was a little tricky wayfinding in the dark, but we managed OK and did not get lost.

We met Sven, his sister, and her friend as we reached the end of the Burgos suburbs. They were pilgrims from Minnesota, where Sven was a retired farmer from the Bemidji area. They were delightful folks. We would see them from time to time all the way to Santiago de Compostela.

Within a couple of hours we entered the *meseta*, or rather, we climbed *up to* the *meseta*.[1] This landform—which comprises 40 percent of the

---

1. While Switzerland has the distinction of being the highest European nation, Spain ranks second, with an average elevation of over 2,000 feet. The Spanish landmass, where not explicitly mountainous, is largely an upland plateau. Cartwright, *Catholic Shrines*, 113.

nation—is actually an elevated plateau. A tree-planting effort has been undertaken along several sections of the Camino in the *meseta*. Perhaps one day they will provide pilgrims with shade.[2] For now, however, they are little more than sticks with a few brownish leaves holding on for dear life. No shade from these trees.

One day these trees will provide a shady *meseta* walk
(GFreihalter/Wikimedia CC BY-SA 3.0)

After an easy stroll of eleven kilometers, we walked into—and rapidly through—the village of Tardajos, population 950. St. Teresa of Ávila—the great mystic saint of the sixteenth century—offered prayers in Tardajos's *Iglesia de Nuestra Señora de la Asunción*.[3] St. Francis of Assisi is said to have stayed in this town during his pilgrimage to St. James in 1214. The overwhelming view of most is that he was indeed a Camino pilgrim. That said, neither of his earliest biographers mention such a pilgrimage, so his purported peregrination to Santiago may fall more into the realm of tradition than historical fact. Be prepared for an argument on this in discussions with Franciscans.

The next village through which we passed was Rabé de las Calzadas. We checked the guidebook before leaving Tardajos just in case there might

2. Kublai Khan allegedly had trees planted along the roads of China to "give solace to travelers." O'Reilly et al., *Best Travel Writing*, 215.

3. Dintaman and Landis, *Hiking the Camino*, 352.

be some point of interest we would regret missing. No such luck, but we did discover this little medieval nugget:[4]

> *De Tardajos a Rabé*
> *no te faltarán trabajos.*
> *Y de Rabé a Tardajos,*
> *liberanos Domine!*

> *From Tardajos to Rabé*
> *you will not lack for troubles.*
> *And from Rabé to Tardajos,*
> *Deliver us, oh Lord!*

The warnings of medieval poets notwithstanding, we enjoyed a pleasant stroll to Rabé de las Calzadas. Just as in Tardajos, there was nothing much to see.

The *meseta* is mostly flat, but not without its charms

The villages on the *meseta* typically do not appear until you are right on top of them, as they are tucked into valleys where the rivers flow. We found ourselves asking, "Where is that village anyway?" And then there it would be. This was the case as Hornillos del Camino popped up like a jack-in-the-box. It seemed that we would have to walk off the edge of the horizon, declare our guidebook and its multicolored maps a fraud when the town finally showed up. As we walked down the *cuesta matamulas* (mule-killing

4. Ayuntamiento de Tardajos, "Camino."

incline) into the valley we ran into Veronica—an older woman walking the wrong way for a pilgrim.[5] We saw so few people walking against the grain that when we did, we reflexively stopped for a chat to ensure that the person was not lost, confused, or just plain cuckoo. Veronica was perhaps seventy years of age. OK, that is generous. She was seventy-five years old if she was a day. She was attired in flowing full-length earth-toned robes. Except for the cowl and wimple, she could have been one of the Felician sisters burdened by God to serve as one of my teachers at Our Lady of Refuge parish school. She informed us that she had walked the Camino six times. This was her last. Indeed, her record of pilgrimage is at least the equal of Chaucer's Wife of Bath—she of *The Canterbury Tales*—who logged pilgrimages to Jerusalem, Rome, Bologna, Santiago de Compostela, and Cologne.[6] In addition to Veronica's Camino addiction, she had also done pilgrimages to Jerusalem, Rome, Assisi, and several other places I cannot recall. To be fair to the Wife of Bath, she *walked* her pilgrimages—when she was not losing her lunch over the side of a Venetian ship. Veronica had the benefit of airplanes. Still, her record was impressive. She wore a brooch from which hung a badge for each of her pilgrimages. It was an impressive bit of hardware, and gave an almost military impression—not unlike a general's chest full of campaign ribbons. Joe made a gentle inquiry as to her views on how the Camino had changed since her first experience so many decades earlier. With this invitation Veronica informed us in strident tones that she was disappointed—bitterly so—with how crowded the Camino had become. The shameless increase in the number of hospitality establishments that had sprung up to support the pilgrims had stripped The Way of its original sense of rugged spiritual struggle and striving. Speaking of The Way, she railed against Martin Sheen and his film *The Way* like a woman truly and utterly scorned. That movie, she declared, was the single greatest impetus for all the tourists on walking holidays that desecrate the pilgrimage to St. James. Terrible. Just as she got really cranked up, she seemed to deflate a bit as if

5. In truth, her name was not Veronica. We never learned her name, but we had to call her something as we walked along discussing the encounter with her. Veronica is a corrupted version of the Latin *vera iconica*—"true icon"—and is the name given to the cloth said to bear the image of Christ's face while being wiped during his walk to Calvary. So great was the devotion to this relic that as many as a dozen pilgrims per day were crushed to death by the crowds when it was exposed in Rome. No wonder, since non-Italian pilgrims gained an indulgence of twelve thousand years remission from Purgatory for each hour of veneration. Italian pilgrims received smaller, but still generous indulgences. Freeman, *Holy Bones*, 211.

6. Chaucer, *Canterbury Tales*, 14–15.

accepting the inevitable and her original calm reasserted itself. She wished us *buen Camino*, pointed her wrinkled face toward the east, and tottered away up the path. While Veronica's six Caminos may sound like a lot—and it certainly is—she was by no means the world record holder in this. A thirteenth-century *peregrino*—the goldsmith Blessed Fazio of Cremona— made pilgrimage to Santiago de Compostela and Rome an amazing eigh- teen times each. One wonders when he had time for goldsmithing.

Eleven long kilometers after briefly scanning the many charms of Hornillos del Camino we entered Hontanas (population sixty-six). We noticed a flyer affixed to a power pole calling pilgrims' attention to a missing man—Dominique Radenac. We had seen these flyers nearly every day since we began our pilgrimage in St. Jean Pied-de-Port. Nobody we spoke with seemed to know anything about him. Was he ill? Abducted? Lost? Thankfully, a question posted about the welfare of this fellow on the Camino de Santiago Forum resulted in a response from a German pilgrim indicating that Mr. Radenac was safe and sound. He never told his family that he was leaving for the Camino. They panicked—understandably—and posted the flyers in the hope that someone would find him. Thankfully, someone did.

**An anxious family took advantage of the Camino's pilgrim network
to reunite with a loved one**

Veronica recommended the Santa Brigida *albergue* in Hontanas, so that is where we ended the day's walk after twenty long miles. We met some South African pilgrims in the *albergue's* bar with whom we enjoyed a friendly chat. The *albergue* offered a shared pilgrim dinner, which was both delicious and convivial. Dinner was accompanied by lots of chatter with Aussies, Italians, Brits, and South Africans. The *hospitalero* and his wife introduced all in attendance to a local character named Victorino. A short, round man—Victorino was one of Hontanas's leading lights. Evidently this fellow was instrumental in the revitalization of the Camino in this area, and for this and other good deeds he was widely esteemed. Camino-building was not Victorino's only skill. To the great amusement of all gathered he showed us how a *porrón* of red wine could be poured on his bald head, where from there it trickled in an apparently controlled way down his nose and into his lower lip, which was jutted forward like an eavestrough. After this demonstration, the *porrón* was passed around the table for others to attempt to duplicate it to the best of their ability, which was uniformly shoddy. To this day, Joe has a red wine stain on his shirt. Having greater esteem for my shirt, I passed.

When I left Burgos I had some regard for the careful bandaging of my blistered toe. The twenty-mile walk did not do it any harm. I committed to tape it up and do eighteen more miles the next day.

My prayers between Burgos and Hontanas were devoted to giving thanks for Damien Jarzembowski's friendship. Though twenty years older than me, he is still a junior high cutup at heart. Always good for a rib-cracking bear hug, I am careful to flex in anticipation of his hearty greetings. I love that guy.

Camino graffiti in Rabé de las Calzadas

Joe and I attended a pilgrim Mass at *Iglesia de la Immaculada Concepción*. At the end of Mass the priest called all of the pilgrims to the front where he presented us each with a small silver cross. It was one of the more moving liturgies we had attended during our pilgrimage.

I was dead tired as I crawled into my lower bunk to end the day. I hoped the women from Texas with whom we were sharing a room would zip it, and soon. Gotta sleep. Gotta sleep. Gotta . . . zzzzzzz.

Our *sello* from Albergue Santa Brigida, Hontanas

Palencian Pedestrians

The midnight bell from the church next door was charming. The 3:00 a.m. bell, less so. The 5:00 a.m. bell was outdone only by the rooster-crowing competition it engendered. Resigned to the many ways *albergues* prevent sleep rather than encourage it, I kept reminding myself to be satisfied with the sleep I needed as opposed to the sleep I wanted. On a bright note, my toe felt better. I taped it up and hoped for the best on the day's eighteen-mile walk.

The bobbing headlamps just behind us as we walked out of a pitch-black Hontanas turned out to be Tony and his wife from Norwich, England. They were charming conversation partners, and all smiles that morning. They told us they had applied for permits that would allow them to work at a college in Papua New Guinea. The required paperwork came through in the middle of the night, and was in their phones when they awoke. They had two weeks to finish the Camino and get to Port Moresby to begin their new life there. We wished them a heartfelt *buen Camino*, and extended our best wishes for every possible success in the next chapter of their lives. Their good fortune powered their pace to a level we could not match, and they were soon far ahead of us. We never saw them again.

The walk from Hontanas to Castrojeriz was perhaps the most pleasant ten kilometers of the pilgrimage thus far. The air was delightfully, refreshingly cool. The path was comfortably level. The sky, filled with stars and a bright moon until the sun began to rise, created a riot of colors as it illumined the *meseta's* terraced hills.

We walked for awhile along the tree-lined road, taking time to investigate the haunting ruins of the *Convento de San Antón*. This eleventh-century convent was reputed to house the relics of St. Anthony, the famous third-century desert hermit. The Camino passed under one of the soaring arches of the now derelict abbey. Joe and I took some time to walk through the ruins, which hosts a no-electricity, no-running water *albergue*. If I ever have the chance to walk another pilgrimage on the Camino, I will do my best to stay in the more out-of-the-way *albergues* like the one tucked into the corner of this fascinating place.

I will sleep in the ruins during my next pilgrimage
(Manuel Velazquez/Wikimedia CC BY 3.0)

As we walked into Castrojeriz we admired the hilltop castle—now in ruins—that guarded the town in former days. Called the *Castillo de San Esteban*, Romans used the castle, thought by some to be founded by Julius Caesar, to protect the roads to Galicia's lucrative gold mines. There is some evidence that the ancient Celts were there first, however. Eventually it was taken over by the Romans, stolen by the Visigoths, borrowed by the Castilians, and is now the home—likely permanent—of the Great Bustard, Tawny Pipit, and other *meseta* winged conquerors.

Our shadows and we walk toward Castrojeriz and its hilltop castle

The Blessed Virgin Mary takes on many different forms for innumerable causes all over the world. Castrojeriz may be the only place where she is honored for a piece of fruit. *Iglesia de Santa María del Manzano* (St. Mary of the Apple) is dedicated to the sudden and understandably surprising appearance of Mary in a Castrojeriz apple tree. Tradition holds that the horse that St. James was riding was spooked—rearing up and landing hard enough to leave hoofprints permanently embedded in the stone pavements.

The received wisdom about the *meseta* is that it is flat. I'd say that it is more *flat-ish* than flat. It is certainly characterized by long views with big, wide skies. But every once in awhile we found ourselves out of breath and perspiring freely as we climbed one or another of the *meseta's* unlikely hills. As we left Castrojeriz and crossed the Ordrilla valley, we positively grunted our way up the impossibly steep *Alto de Mostelares*. The climb was only thirty minutes in duration, but it was at 18 percent grade, the day was heating up, and required a few prayers to get me to the top. The view from the top back toward Castrojeriz was priceless.

Just before Itero de Vega we passed out of the province of Burgos and into Palencia. Each of these border crossings gives us a sense of accomplishment. The first Spanish university—and one of the earliest universities anywhere—was established in Palencia (and now enlightens young minds in neighboring Valladolid). Palencia is noted for its barley, wheat, sugar beets, hemp, linen and woolen clothes, porcelain, leather, paper, and rugs. One of the province's principal locales is Aguilar de Campoo—a place that *Wikipedia* bizarrely described as "a biscuit and tourist village."[7] You can imagine our excitement at crossing the border into this seeming wonderland.

Welcome to Palencia

One of the interesting aspects of the Camino de Santiago is the degree to which The Way had been festooned with graffiti of every imaginable style, degree of sophistication, aesthetic, and level of philosophical merit. While there were certainly exceptions, Camino graffiti seemed to be of three distinct types. The first might be thought of as artwork. Credit must be given where it is due, for the panache that some possess in wielding a can of spray paint is impressive indeed. Some of it was actually beautiful. The second kind of Camino graffiti fell into the category of "prayer intentions." We saw daily reminders of pilgrims who, with little else but a Sharpie and a hope in divine intervention, left their mark on road signs, Camino markers, and other accommodating flat surfaces. Finally—and in some ways most interestingly—was the graffiti that fell squarely in the category of "bullshit Camino philosophy." This was ubiquitous on the road to St. James.[8]

7. Wikipedia, s.v. "Province of Palencia," last modified January 26, 2022, https://en.wikipedia.org/wiki/Province_of_Palencia.

8. Graffiti has been left by pilgrims in holy places since ancient times and predates Christianity by millennia. For an excellent review of religious graffiti down through the

I bought a sandwich for lunch in Itero de Vega. Called a *bocadillo* in Spanish, these sandwiches were typically a twelve-inch loaf of crusty white bread with a modest, nay—miniscule—filling of chorizo, cheese, Serrano ham, or tuna. Joe and I decided that if we were in charge of things, we'd require our Spanish friends to add some tomato, onion, mayonnaise, and mustard. *Bocadillos* were decidedly dry. As dust. No, on second thought, the moisture content of dust is higher than a *bocadillo*. My deepest and most sincere apologies to all dust, everywhere.

Joe croaks a request for water while enjoying his *bocadillo*

The *meseta* offered long periods of quiet, with little change in the landscape. Joe and I resorted to several activities that helped the miles pass enjoyably. We sang songs, or at least the parts we knew. We prayed the Rosary every day, being sure to offer these prayers for our special intentions. And today between Itero de Vega and Boadilla del Camino we composed lyrics to the tune of "The Twelve Days of Christmas," each of which reflected some aspect of our journey. Our ears bled as we sang our way across the endless miles.

The day's walk was dedicated to my gratitude for Ray and Sue Smith. For thirty-four years they have befriended me, guided me, supported me, and served as fine role models. I am glad to have them in my life, and looked forward to seeing them again when I returned home.

We never knew exactly where we were going to sleep. Our preference was to avoid booking ahead because it tied us down to having to make

centuries, see Ragazzoli et al., *Scribbling through History*, 37–47.

it to a particular town, even if we wanted to stop early or go farther. But without making reservations it was always a bit of a crapshoot to know if there would be room at the inn. This was the cause of some anxiety, but we'd been lucky and had no problems. When we walked into the *albergue* in Boadilla—"En El Camino"—and asked if there were two beds available, Eduardo, the *hospitalero*, gave us a big smile and replied, "Why not?!" I was relieved to receive this response, for Boadilla del Camino was a mere speck on the map. The yard of the *albergue* was chockablock with pilgrims, and I was afraid we had arrived too late to secure beds. Still, the Camino provided—once again.

We shared a room in Boadilla del Camino with Reinhardt from Germany and two fellows from the Basque Country. They were very clear to tell us that they were from the Basque Country as opposed to Spain, Navarre, Pamplona, etc. We grew accustomed to this, as our fellow Spanish *peregrinos* had a decidedly regional identity.

We wandered around Boadilla del Camino after attending to our grooming, hygiene, and laundry. There really was not much to see. Only 124 souls call that place home. Just around the corner from the *albergue* stood a pillar, the *Rollo de la Justicia*. This was erected to symbolize the independence granted by the king to Boadilla in the fifteenth century. Along with the ability to exercise some limited degree of local self-government, the pillar stands as witness to the town's newfound permission to publicly torture and hang its own criminals. Boadillians through the ages have no doubt swelled with pride at the honor. We were very glad indeed to make it through the evening without witnessing the local burgesses' authority employed to such a purpose.

The *Rollo de la Justicia*

Boadilla del Camino was, in so many ways, typical of the countless rural hamlets through which we had walked since setting out from St. Jean Pied-de-Port. People lived in these places, but we very rarely saw them. Surely there must have been residents who populated the houses, tilled the fields, brought in the crops, tended the livestock, prayed in the church, sent children to school, and observed the seasons with festive celebrations. Seemingly absent was the vibrant hum of life one might have wished to find. More than one-fifth of the Spanish population lives in rural villages like Boadilla del Camino. Rural areas like this constitute 94 percent of the Spanish landmass.[9] Rural tourism has seen an increase in the provinces through which we walked,[10] but perhaps this has not been enough to sustain a vibrant community life among rural folk.

Dinner tonight was a shared pilgrim experience. We shared the table with Reinhardt and Heide from Germany (not to be confused with the other Reinhardt from Germany who was one of our roommates for the evening). Retired seventy-somethings who spend the winters in Spain, they did not speak much English, so we had an evening full of hand gestures, charades, Google Translate, and fun-filled miscommunication. Heide had back surgery to correct a spinal stenosis in 2015. The year before that she underwent quintuple bypass surgery. In 2016 she was walking the Camino. Amazing. This was Reinhardt's fifth Camino. These sweet people would become friends with whom we would share much of the remaining pilgrimage.

If I was reading my maps correctly, we would be halfway through our pilgrimage by the end of the walk the following day. I could hardly believe that we had made such progress. Nearly 250 miles! Was my heart 50 percent healed by that point in the pilgrimage? Time would tell.

Albergue En El Camino stamp

9. Cervantes-Godoy, "Role of Agriculture."

10. 6.4% in Navarre, 1% in La Rioja, 17% in Castilla y León, and 6% in Galicia. Canoves, "Rural Tourism."

Tierra de Campos

The walk out of Boadilla del Camino was very dark. As the sun began to brighten the eastern horizon the colors bedazzled us, with a crescent moon to make the heavens even more stunning.

The sixteen-mile walk to Carrión de los Condes was pancake flat. The main route ran along a busy highway and was very *meseta*-like. We took an alternate route that guided us along the Rio Ucieza, offered shade, and lacked the noisy intrusions of passing vehicles. It was altogether pleasant.

Before the sun rose too high in the sky I offered prayers dedicated to the spiritual intention of today's walk—my friendship with Jim and Martie Bultman. They have been so supportive and kind over such a long time. Jim has been a significant sponsor of my career. I owe him a lot. God bless them both.

Camino sculpture on the way to Carrión de los Condes

After a delightfully brisk walk of about six kilometers, we came to Fromista, where we pulled over for a *cafe con leche*. Fromista was home to an interesting dam system—part of the Canal de Castilla, which carries water to the *meseta* from the Cantabrian Mountains to the north and west. Constructed between 1753 and 1849, the canal was intended to bring goods from Santander on the Bay of Biscay to the cereal-growing regions of Castile. The railroad came along, however, and mule-pulled barges became obsolete before the plan could be fully implemented. We ended up walking along the canal for quite a while, and it was delightful. Trees, birds, and

113

waterfowl abounded near the watercourse. Alas, our arrival in Fromista was too early in the day for a tour of its cheese museum. Next time. For sure.

Thirty minutes of lamentful walking occasioned by our disappointment at missing out on the wonders of Fromista's cheese museum were rewarded when we stumbled upon Población de Campos, population 140. You may be wondering what the "de Campos" appendage on this municipality's name signifies. Población and most of the other communities of the province of Palencia are part of a geographical region known as *Tierra de Campos* (Land of Fields). This is the dryland-farming, cereal-growing region of the *meseta*. It straddles several administrative areas in addition to Palencia, including sections of León, Zamora, and Valladolid. Originally it was known as "Gothic Plains" (*Campi Gothici* or *Campi Gothorum*), because the Visigoths settled there after the Franks gave them the heave-ho out of Gaul.[11] The Visigoths have given way to local tourism boards that now produce YouTube videos extolling the many charms of these otherwise unremarkable places. "We have *two albergues!*" exclaims Bercianos del Real Camino. "Pfft," counters El Burgo Ranero contemptuously, "we have *three albergues!* And a *supermercado!*"

Really, how is a pilgrim to choose given the dizzying array of attractive options?

**Typical Tierra de Campos landscape with traditional *palomar*
(Xauxa [Håkan Svensson]/Wikimedia CC BY-SA 3.0)**

11. Diputación de Palencia, "Tierra de Campos," https://palenciaturismo.es/en/node/890.

We had a decision to make in Población de Campos. Should we follow the primary Camino route next to the noisy highway? Or should we take the alternative route—less well marked and 1.5 kilometers longer—that ran next to the Río Ucieza alongside delightfully shaded groves populated by tweeting birds that flit playfully from branch to branch? We turned right and followed the alternate route toward Villovieco. Once there we came upon an increasingly common Camino amenity—the pathside pilgrim rest stop. These thoughtfully placed parks typically contained a couple of picnic tables and a fountain with refreshing, potable water. They were normally shaded by trees, and offered a comfortable place to stop, air feet, have a snack, rehydrate, and set-a-spell. In the case of Villovieco we were also treated to a playful sculpture of *Santiago Peregrino*. Regrettably, too many pilgrims treated these parks poorly, causing blooms of the invasive species, *toiletpapericus everywhereicus*. The "Leave No Trace" ethic seemed to be less well known on the Camino than one desired.

The Camino led us to the next dot on the map, Villalcázar de Sirga. The town was home to the stupendous *Iglesia de Santa María la Blanca* and its "White Virgin"—reputed to be the source of many miracles. A playful statue of *Santiago Peregrino* sat at a table in the church's courtyard, encouraging pilgrims to rest awhile and consider the glories of the intricately carved portico.

St. James pays no attention to this pilgrim in Villalcázar de Sirga

Joe and I split a pork loin and pimiento *bocadillo* for lunch. Pimiento was a popular vegetable in the *Tierra de Campos*, and was used on sandwiches, in *tortillas*, and other dishes. It was tasty, and helped moisten the otherwise dry Spanish sandwiches.

Joe's eagle eye and keen sense of direction keeps us on the right track

We walked for a while with Lisa from Madison, Wisconsin. Just laid off from her job as a tour operator, she was out traveling some of the places she used to help book for clients while she figured out what came next in her life. She was a delightful person, and a scholarship rower for the University of Wisconsin during her college days, which gave us lots to discuss in the world of sports. In some ways, Lisa was just like so many other young adults we met on the Camino—charming people searching for what was next in their lives—and maybe for what was important. For a sense of vocation.

One of the delights that draws pilgrims to Carrión de los Condes is the chance to benefit from the hospitality of the singing nuns of the convent of Santa Maria. The *albergue* they operate offers an evening liturgy complete with a lively guitar-infused hymn sing. Imagine our disappointment when I called ahead to try to book beds in their *albergue* only to be told that, and here I quote directly, "*Lo siento, el albergue está cerrado hoy*" (I'm sorry, the hostel is closed today). Huh? *Albergues* are a bit like hotels in that they are open or they are closed, but they do not normally take days off. Later we learned—directly from one of the singing nuns herself—that the convent only operates the *albergue* in season. We arrived too late in the year. Shucks.

Our disappointment was assuaged when we checked into our second choice—the Albergue Espiritu Santo, a former convent run by the

Daughters of Charity of St. Vincent DePaul. Beyond the evident kindness of the sisters who ran the place, we were cheered by the fact that this place had no bunk beds. No climbing up or down for us tonight. Pilgriming helps one to appreciate the little graces in life.

We went through our normal *albergue*-arrival routine. My *Español* isn't great—and it gets worse the more fatigued I am. But I do know the difference between *señoras* and *caballeros*. Imagine my surprise when I stumbled numbly into the ladies shower room. Well, they were very kind about the whole thing as I beat a sheepish, red-faced retreat.

Carrión de los Condes celebrates the feast of its patron, San Zolian, every June 27. There was a monastery on the west side of town named for him. Well, it used to be a monastery. Now it's a swanky hotel. On June 27 the locals pack into the *plaza mayor* as an image of the saint is carried in procession to the church while all gathered sing lustily if not well the anthem that honors the town:[12]

> *¡Gloria al pueblo que ha dado a Castilla*
> *poetas ilustres e infanzones de pro!*
> *Con orgullo y honor sin mancilla*
> *lancemos el grito de ¡Viva Carrión!*
>
> *Tu nombre cantan las aguas del río,*
> *leyendas moras pregonan tu fe,*
> *que hizo ermita un castillo bravío*
> *para amar a la Virgen de Belén.*
>
> *En tus casas señoriales,*
> *albergue de comuneros,*
> *aún refulgen tus aceros*
> *con destellos inmortales.*
>
> *Y, celoso soberano*
> *de tu gloria y tu panera,*
> *hoy defiendes la bandera*
> *del labriego castellano.*
>
> *Glory to the people who have given to Castile*
> *illustrious poets and men of birth!*
> *With pride and honor without blemish*
> *let's launch the cry of ¡Viva Carrión!*

12. Ayuntamiento de Carrión de los Condes, "Himno-Carrión."

Your name sing the waters of the river,
black legends proclaim your faith,
which made a brave castle chapel
to love the Virgin of Bethlehem.

In your stately homes,
hostel of commoners,
still shine your steels
with immortal flashes.

And, jealous sovereign
of your glory and your bread basket,
today you defend the flag
of the Castilian peasant.

Is this exactly what the anthem speaks of? Hard to say. Google Translate thinks so, but I am not laying any wagers that it is one hundred percent on the money. In any case, Joe and I were on the lookout for shining steels flashing immortally.

We went to the pilgrim Mass at the church of Santa Maria. We were welcomed so warmly by both the priest and by the nuns of the convent of Santa Maria, who provided each of us with a small paper star to "light our way to Compostela." This was a very powerful blessing I will not soon forget.

The four nuns who serve as *hospitaliteras* in Albergue Espíritu Santo were so very kind, thoughtful, and generous. One example of their charity toward pilgrims was on display at bedtime. A few minutes before 10:00 as people in our bunk room were settling in for the night, one of the sisters came into the room and walked from bed to bed personally wishing each pilgrim a good night's sleep. This was lovely, and was made even kinder when, while chatting with the young woman in the bed next to me, she noticed the look of distress on this *peregrina's* face. The older Spanish fellow who occupied the bed adjacent to hers was already fast asleep, and was snoring like a jet engine. I am sure the young woman was wondering if she would get any sleep at all with such a horrific noise just a few feet away. The sister assessed the situation perfectly, however. She shook the man until he awoke with a loud snort. His eyes flew open as he looked up to see the face of a seventy-five-year-old nun looking down at him. "*Buenas noches, peregrino. ¡Duermas bien!*"[13] whispered Sister as she glanced over at the young woman and winked. International snoring incident averted.

Hospitality for pilgrims—even from ecclesiastical persons—was not something that medieval pilgrims could always count on, despite the injunctions of the Church in earlier times that "pilgrims are to be received into our houses, as the Lord has written."[14] While those in charge of pilgrimage destinations were obviously keen on lots of pilgrimage-inspired traffic (and the cash it brought in),[15] others were sometimes hostile to pilgrims, and treated them as vagrants who ought to be improving their spiritual state at home and not rambling abroad. The Dutch priest and scholar Erasmus, while thoroughly Catholic in his commitments, was just as thoroughly Reformed in his views regarding pilgrimage, arguing that the wise pilgrim moves from room to room ensuring good order in his own house as a way to ensure spiritual fitness.[16] Eleven hundred years before Erasmus the Roman poet Rutilius Claudius Namatianus leveled similar criticism against Christian hermits who roamed the countryside of Gaul seeking a closer spiritual connection with God.[17]

I was feeling some homesickness. It was not unexpected. The older I get the more I long for the generative presence of hearth and home, kith and kin. I prayed that I could check this painful emotion. It had been a long time since I had seen my family, but I tried to find solace in the idea that each day I walked brought me closer to being reunited with those I love.

We loved the Albergue Espíritu Santo and the sisters who treated us so well

13. Good night, Pilgrim. Sleep well!

14. McNeill and Gamer, *Medieval Handbooks*, 93.

15. In 1220, the shrine of St. Thomas Becket at Canterbury in England brought in £1,142, two-thirds of the cathedral's income. Freeman, *Holy Bones*, 7.

16. Erasmus, *Colloquies*, 650.

17. Wikipedia, s.v. "Rutilius Claudius Namatianus," last modified February 25, 2022, https://en.wikipedia.org/wiki/Rutilius_Claudius_Namatianus.

The Roman Road

I slept well in the convent-*albergue* Espíritu Santo despite the Snoring Spaniard grinding the very air of the bunkroom. Joe was sleeping soundly when I shook him awake at 6:00. Snoring Spaniard was a nuisance for him as well during the night. By this point our early morning movements were as efficient and well-choreographed as soldiers on campaign, and we bid goodbye to the convent where we were so hospitably accommodated.

We crept over the Rio Carrión, past the Royal Monastery of San Zoilo, and out of Carrión de los Condes under cover of darkness. It was cold enough that we could see our breath. The sky was positively illumined by heavenly bodies, including the constellation Orion with his belt of three stars. The moon was a sliver, and as the sky eventually brightened it hung over a riot of colors produced by the rising sun. Another beautiful morning for a walk.

We typically shared the path with other early risers. An observer might conclude that a firefly hatch was underway as our headlamps bobbed up and down in a long string for a mile or so. Joe and I had come to rely on other pilgrims' sense of direction and wayfinding during those darkened hours of the pre-dawn. That morning was no different, but the fellow we were trailing was less than certain about which way to go in the dark. His uncertainty infected us, and we wandered for a bit before eventually finding the correct route.

When there is no town for seventeen kilometers, you eat breakfast where you can

We walked along the old Roman road—the *Via Aquitana*—out of Carrión de los Condes for seventeen boring kilometers before reaching anything that resembled civilization. The road was straight as a string. Our guidebook warned us about this long stretch, so we were prepared with breakfast, lunch, snacks, and plenty of water in our packs. The *Via Aquitana* is a third-century road designed according to Roman engineering standards and intended to ensure easy access to Galician gold mines. Built a bit higher than the surrounding fields to prevent flooding and freezing, the road appears flat but is actually crowned a bit and bordered by ditches to encourage drainage. The Romans were able to build such straight roads by employing a tool called a *groma*, two wooden segments connected at right angles from which dangled lead weights.[18]

A preserved section of a Roman road (Adriano Pucciarelli/Upsplash)

The long walk between Carrión de los Condes and Calzadilla de la Cueza was dusty, sunny, and flyblown. It might have been boring, except for the fact that 5.1 kilometers out of Carrión we officially passed the halfway point of the Camino. This provided us with a pleasant sense of accomplishment. We stopped to mark the moment with a selfie, then turned our faces west and kept trudging.

We walked behind Reinhardt and Heide for a few miles. It was touching to see these aging retirees walking to Santiago de Compostela hand-in-hand like teenagers. We also chatted with Brock and Sue while

18. Trueman, "Roman Roads."

plodding along. South African immigrants to Perth, Australia, they were delightful folks with whom we would enjoy many engaging conversations. Sue was a retired high school history teacher who still substituted from time to time. Brock owned a small business applying tinting to auto glass. They felt lucky that their son's family also immigrated to Australia—to Brisbane—and were only five hours by airplane from them. It was one more reminder of how lucky Carol and I are to have our kids and grandkids so close. What a blessing. May we never take it for granted.

The seemingly endless *Via Aquitana* eventually tipped us into Calzadilla de la Cueza, where we were delighted to see that the municipal *albergue* offered a sunny cafe. Weary from our morning's exertions, we settled in, removed shoes and socks, and enjoyed a rejuvenating beverage. And a sandwich. Perhaps two sandwiches. And a second refreshing beverage.

Well-fortified after our Calzadilla pit stop, we hit the road for the final stretch of the day's journey. Our destination was Terradillos de los Templarios—a mere seven kilometers down the dirt road. On the way we passed through Ledigos. If it is possible to hear a village snore, Ledigos is where this could be observed. Calzadilla was sleepy. Ledigos, comatose.

Not much shade on the meseta

We pulled into Terradillos de los Templarios ("small Templar terraces") with its population of seventy-eight around 3:00 after a seventeen-mile day. Our *albergue*—"Jacques de Molay"—was named after the last Grand Master of the Knights Templar. The Knights Templar (a.k.a. Poor Fellow-Soldiers of Christ and of the Temple of Solomon, a.k.a. Order of Solomon's Temple, a.k.a. The Templars) were a Catholic military order founded in 1119 and disbanded in 1312. The Templars were responsible for safeguarding pilgrims. The order had both martial and noncombatant members. While the Templars are largely remembered for their military skill and crusading acumen, they are less frequently remembered for establishing what amounted to a string of banks spanning Europe all the way to the Holy Land. They became very powerful as they grew wealthier. Temporal rulers like Phillip IV of France came to rely on the Templars to finance their various projects, wars, and other regal escapades. Philip, being uninterested in paying off his Templar loans, instead decided to purge the order, and in 1307 rounded up the leaders and burned them at the stake on trumped-up charges of heresy. While this may have put paid to the Templars as an organization, it was also effective in cementing their legendary status in the imaginations of adoring millions even unto the present day.[19]

The story of the Templars is a good reminder that we should cloak ourselves in humility. One day they were champions of the Crusades and as rich as Croesus, and the next they are remembered by a pilgrim hostel in a flyspeck town in the middle of nowhere.

The Templars and their terrible, horrible, no-good, very bad day
(Bibliothèque Municipale, Besançon, France. Erich Lessing/Art Resource, NY/
Wikimedia (Public Domain)

19. Barber, *New Knighthood*, 314–34.

When we checked in to the *albergue* I noticed a desk with a sign that read, "Massages." I thought it was just Spanglish for messages, but no. The *hospitalero* was a massage therapist. Just one more day of flawless communication with Gringo Rich and his sidekick Smilin' Joe.

As afternoon gave way to evening gloaming, we sought refuge from the day's exertions in our beds, where I was reminded of Wendell Berry's assertion: "There comes . . . a longing never to travel again except on foot."[20]

Our pilgrim passports record our stay at Albergue Jacques De Molay

Soledad, Our Guardian Angel

As I sat under a star spangled 6:00 a.m. sky in the *albergue's* courtyard waiting for Joe to emerge, I found myself giving thanks for this good-natured friend. He was a terrific pilgrim-partner. He balanced me perfectly. When I was in a hurry to get to the next place, he went a bit slower and we saw more as a result. While I am a bit introverted, Joe—while naturally quiet—had "*Hola. Buenos Dias. Buen Camino*" on his lips for every single person we encountered. And if they spoke English—and maybe even if they didn't—he asked how they were, if they were enjoying the day, where they were from, etc. He was a collector of souls, that guy. I did not thank him often enough for his friendship.

The first habitation we encountered on the day's walk was Greater Metropolitan Moratinos, population sixty-eight. It was in Moratinos that we observed a very interesting type of building characteristic of *Tierra de Campos* communities. The *bodega* is a kind of underground cellar originally

20. Berry, *Remembering*, 87.

intended to store the locality's produce—wine, cheese, mushrooms, grain, etc. Nowadays they serve as gathering places for families and friends. They resemble Hobbit houses, with doors installed on hillsides from which chimneys (and sometimes TV antennas) protrude. One expected Bilbo Baggins to emerge chewing on a pipe while nervously fingering a suspicious ring engraved with Old Elvish. . . .

Moratinos *bodega*

The built environment was beginning to change. There was less stone in this part of Spain, so buildings tended to be constructed from bricks or adobe. The churches and other ancient structures were beginning to reflect the influence of Moorish architecture common during the time when much of Spain was Islamic. This *mudéjar* style was noticeably different from either the Romanesque or Gothic architecture that had dominated our Camino experience to that point. I was grateful in some ways to see this influence as we strolled through towns and villages, for it was a reminder of the many ways that the nine-hundred-year Muslim presence in Spain shaped the Spanish social imaginary in the present day, including the Spanish "memory" of St. James in his role as *Santiago Matamoros* as opposed to the Galilean fisherman who, when invited to "come and see" did just that. The Islamic history of Spain is incredibly rich and multilayered. Today about 4 percent of the population is Muslim, but most of these people are immigrants and not descendants of the medieval Moors who converted to

Christianity (or were forcibly expelled) during the reign of Ferdinand and Isabella in the fifteenth century.

Iglesia de San Lorenzo in Sahagún with its *mudéjar* architecture

After a ten-kilometer stroll, we came to the Ermita Virgen del Puente, a small *mudéjar* chapel situated in a lovely grove next to a bridge over the Río Valderaduey. The church was not much to look at, but one hundred yards or so to the south stood the ruins of an ancient gate. One of the pillars of this gate was decorated with a very buff St. Francis of Assisi holding his "rule" which instructs monks to pray and work—*ora et labora*. Some pilgrims consider this gate to be the "official" halfway point of the *Camino Frances*. At least one Camino blogger thought the gate is the entrance to Middle Earth's Mordor.[21] In any case, the actual midpoint of the Camino is a subject of terrific debate. Some claim that once you have reached Terradillos you are halfway there. These are fighting words to others who claim Sahagún as the halfway mark. Why the hubbub about the location of the Camino's midpoint? Nobody knows.

21. Guest [deleted member 34316], forum post, February 28, 2016, https://www. caminodesantiago.me/community/threads/mid-way-point-on-cf.38633/#post-382400.

St. Francis welcomes pilgrims at the Camino's midpoint. More or less.

The first community of any size we encountered that day was Sahagún. This place was important in medieval times. Only the city of León was bigger in King Alfonso VI's kingdom of the same name. Even now it has nearly three thousand inhabitants, which makes it a metropolis by *Tierra de Campos* standards. We had one of our more memorable Camino moments in Sahagún. The town has many wonderful churches. Joe hated to walk past a church, monastery, convent, or other ecclesial structure without a look around. We decided to explore a bit as we walked through the city so we could see these marvelous monuments. This required us to deviate from the Camino route, leaving the scallop shell markers for awhile as we consulted the guidebook's maps. We must have had our "confused tourist" faces on full display as we stood on a street corner looking, first right and then left, for the landmark that would take us to *Iglesia de San Lorenzo*. A Spanish grandma—Soledad—spotted us from across the street. Thinking us hopelessly lost, she began waving her arms wildly overhead and pointing the way back to the Camino. We gave her our best *Dumb and Dumber* smiles in return, waved with what we thought was sufficient gratitude, and returned to our maps. This caused her to gesticulate even more vigorously, using an overhead, two-arm directional motion common to airport tarmac employees and traffic cops. We shouted our thanks with even more enthusiasm, offering smiles akin to Lewis Carroll's Cheshire Cat.

At this point—thinking us either lost or addled—she hustled, bandy-legged in her flowery housedress, across the street to guide us personally back to the True Way. I used all my flawlessly pronounced, impeccably conjugated Spanish to explain that we did not desire to return to the Camino at that particular moment in time, but instead wished to deviate from the path to enjoy her fair city's monumental churches. Not surprisingly, my perfectly clear explanation offered in precise Castilian Spanish had little effect on this determined do-gooder. If anything, she spoke to us at increased volume, perhaps assuming that we were hard of hearing. By now we had sussed out the direction to the first church. As we offered even more effusive *gracias* and turned to walk away, Soledad—now convinced that we were committing a kind of disrespect to St. James—grasped my wrist with an icy claw of surprising strength and began pulling me in the opposite direction, all the while insisting that her way was best. I whispered to Joe that, under the circumstances, we ought to just let Soledad have her way with us. Sahagún was a small town. How far astray could she lead us? Still firmly affixed to my wrist, she dragged us for a few blocks back the way from which we had just come. She chattered away—at volume—the entire time, pointing out various points of interest and occasions of civic pride. We finally stumbled across a scallop shell marking the Camino's path. She released my wrist from her iron grip, smiled broadly, and with a sweep of her arm pointed us in the direction we were trying so hard to avoid. We put our Cheshire Cat grins on again and through clenched teeth offered *muchisimas gracias*. We walked a block or two down the Camino until she averted her watchful gaze, then beat a speedy detour in the direction of the churches we were so anxious to see. Another international incident avoided.

While walking through Sahagún's *plaza mayor* we ran into François from Quebec City. We had seen François a few times in recent days but had not had the chance to properly introduce ourselves. We would spend several pleasant hours with him before reaching Santiago de Compostela. He asked if we knew where the tourist information center was located, but we weren't sure. I had half a mind to send him back to the street corner where we encountered Soledad, for surely she could direct him if she didn't instinctively boomerang him back to the Camino as she had with us. During our conversation with François we learned that he started his Camino in Le Puy, France, and had been walking for two months. I calculated that he had already walked 750 miles, which made my pilgrimage feel puny by comparison.

Earlier in this account I described the various confraternities that support pilgrims on the Camino. In Sahagún we encountered a local version that occasioned our interest because of an interesting sculpture outside its front door. There was quite a bit of interesting Camino-themed sculpture in the villages, towns, and cities through which we walked. In Sahagún we came across two apparent Klansmen in bronze standing in front of the local headquarters of the Confraternity of Jesus the Nazorean. This brotherhood was established in the sixteenth century and exists to promote the faith by maintaining the chapel adjacent to its office and sponsoring floats in the annual Holy Week processions—which are a big deal in this part of the world. And the hoods? Red hoods on statues and procession participants are *capirotes*—worn as a symbol of penitence by members of Spanish brotherhoods.

I have a memory from my days as a Catholic schoolboy at Our Lady of Refuge parish school. Every year Sister would march us through the hallways and into the church, where we would take turns approaching the altar. Once there the priest—likely one of the Polish imports from Sts. Cyril and Methodius Seminary across the street—would hold crossed (unlit) candles to our throats while intoning the following prayer:

> *Through the intercession of St Blaise, bishop and martyr, may God deliver you from ailments of the throat and from every other evil. In the name of the Father, and of the Son and of the Holy Spirit.*[22]

I had not thought about this in years—decades, really—until we walked into *Iglesia de San Tirso* and saw a sculpture of my old friend, St. Blaise, patron saint of those with throat illnesses.

St. Blaise, who looks like he could benefit from a throat blessing of his own

22. "Throat Blessing of St Blaise," https://www.daily-prayers.org/angels-and-saints/prayers-to-st-blaise/.

We chose to take an alternative route for the afternoon—one that took us away from the busy main road and into Calzadilla de los Hermanillos for the evening by way of the ancient Roman road—the *Via Trajana*. The Romans had to bring many thousands of tons of stone from great distances to build the roadbed up above the level of the winter floods and freezes. Joe and I commented that they should have simply looked to their right or their left at the endless fields filled with rocks. Stupid Romans. Most of the thousands of square miles of wheat fields through which we walked in the *meseta* were very rocky, with an evident lack of topsoil. In some places it appeared that the farmers had simply disked the stones into neat, orderly rows. Even the vineyards of the more verdant La Rioja through which we had walked earlier seem to spring from the living stones. Sven—the farmer from northern Minnesota we met just past Burgos—bemoaned the lack of care for the soil and the impact on this potentially rich agricultural land. James Michener claims that the medieval class system relegated farmers to the lowest castes while allowing gentlemen of privilege to own massive herds of sheep.[23] The sheepherder's guild—the *Mesta*—was given royal license to run its sheep without barrier or respect of property across the entire *meseta*. The value of Merino wool gave Spain a monopoly that some allege prevented the kinds of economic diversification that characterized much of the rest of Europe—even well into the nineteenth century. Whether the suboptimal soil conditions we observed were the legacy of this historico-cultural phenomenon was an interesting thing to ponder. Things seem to change very slowly indeed in Spain.

In medieval days people would regularly get lost in this section of the *meseta*, unable to find their way without natural geographic features. I suppose it must have been a bit like trying to find the corner in a round room. But Joe and I just followed the sun and eventually arrived in Calzadilla de los Hermanillos—our destination for the evening. The municipal *albergue* was tended by a Polish *hospitalatero* who was breaking in a new volunteer who would assume the role of *El Jefe* in just a few days. And besides these two gentlemen we had the entire *albergue* to ourselves with the lone exception of Brock and Sue, who arrived a couple of hours after us. The night before the place was reportedly overflowing with pilgrims, with some relegated to sleeping on mats on the floor. The Camino—and the Holy Spirit—continued to provide for us.

---

23. Michener, *Iberia*, 284–88.

Most *albergues* have rules designed to keep the houses clean and as free as possible from the scourge of bedbugs. Our Polish host was stern indeed on issues of cleanliness, and would not allow us to even bring our backpacks into the building, insisting instead that we keep them in black trash bags on the porch. After a shower and laundry, we ate dinner with Brock and Sue at one of the two restaurants in town. Our first nineteen kilometers the next day were through the country—a section with no towns, no water, no services. Nothing. We bought bread, cheese, and fruit from the local *tienda* to get us through.

The day's prayer intentions were for the sick and dying people I knew—a list of perhaps fifteen people. I hoped God would give each what he or she needed during a stressful time. As I prepared for bed I was reminded of how lucky I am, and in so many ways. This walk was helping me regain a sense of perspective. While the previous six months had been very difficult, it was getting easier to count and name my blessings. I was hoping for a good night of sleep, which would also be a blessing.

Joe and I had this place to ourselves

Big Sky Country

Allison sent me new photos and a video of Kennedy during the night. These and a note from Carol filled my heart and made crawling from my sleeping sack and beginning the daily process of packing up a pleasure. Because Joe and I were the only pilgrims in the lower level of the *albergue* we could turn the light on as we packed. When you had walked as far as we had, the small luxuries made all the difference.

The *albergue* offered a "breakfast" of instant coffee and a packaged muffin that would leave a parakeet still hungry. Well, this would have to do until we took a break later that morning.

It had rained with some force during the night. It was rather amazing that we had walked for nearly three weeks and had not gotten wet. We were lucky, lucky, lucky. Our sleep was interrupted in the night with loud explosions in this otherwise moribund town. We think it was fireworks set off by some teenager bored out of his skull with farmwork.

Looking back at the rising sun as we leave Calzadilla de los Hermanillos

It was hard to believe that we had walked through September and were now into October. The walk began with an eighteen-kilometer section on the old Roman *Via Trajana* through the countryside. For four hours we encountered no people, no cars, no paved roads, no buildings, no town, no bathrooms, and no coffee shops. We did experience a lovely sunrise, a bright blue sky, clouds that seemed the product of a master artist's watercolor brush, fields of wheat swaying gently in the cool breeze, groves of poplar trees, and canals channeling water from the Cantabrian Mountains to the arid *meseta*. Speaking of mountains, the Irago range of the Cantabrians was much closer, and the work we would have to do once we got past León and entered Galicia loomed ahead.

The Cantabrian Mountains begin to emerge on the horizon

We met a man walking alone in the opposite direction near the end of our initial eighteen-kilometer stretch. We greeted him with the usual *buenos dias* and he responded in Michigander English, "And good morning to you." Dennis was from Harbor Springs—a town a few hours north of where Joe and I live. When we had coffee with him in Reliegos a little while later we learned that his company manufactures those wooden maps of lakes that are so prevalent in Michigan gift shops—especially in tourist towns. His knees would not allow him to walk the Camino in the usual manner, so he drove a rental car and met his wife and friends at various places. They were doing the Camino first class—staying in Paradors (Spain's swanky, government-owned hotels) and other luxury accommodations.

This was a welcome sight after eighteen long kilometers

We finished our twenty-four-kilometer walk and arrived in Mansilla de las Mulas ("small estate of the mules") at 12:45. My guidebook directed us to Albergue Gaia as the best of three options. It was a very nice hostel, especially for only five euros. It had a nice kitchen that we used to make our tuna fish sandwich lunch. Joe—who had been craving jam for his bread since our arrival in Spain—found a jar of strawberry preserves in the fridge and dove right in. His day was made. We met Andy and Carrie from Melbourne along with Pam from New Hampshire. They seemed very nice indeed. We would end up spending some time with Pam on the road as our pilgrimage continued.

Had I felt like this from time to time? Indeed, I had.

I had been hungry since we began our walk many weeks before. If there was a basket of bread on the table—and there always was—I would eat it all and ask for a refill. I was concerned that I might be gaining weight because I was rarely without something to nibble on. Well, Albergue Gaia had a scale. I had lost five pounds. I wouldn't mind losing another five before Santiago de Compostela. Once I got home, however, strict dietary discipline would be needed or I would balloon up like the *Hindenburg*.

We made a reservation for a hotel in León, which we'd reach the next day after a short eleven-mile walk. The Hotel Sercotel Alfonso V is near the cathedral, looked very comfortable, and we got a good deal—fifty-nine dollars per night. We planned to stay two nights. We were both looking forward to a rest day.

Joe and I searched for a pre-dinner adult beverage in this pleasant town of nearly two thousand people. We had a beer with Laura and Pam, and then dinner with Brock and Sue, with whom we exchanged email addresses. We also exchanged email addresses with Laura, Heide, and Reinhard. I looked forward to staying in touch with these *peregrinos*.

Mansilla can boast of at least two sources of civic pride. First, it has maintained much of its encircling medieval walls, with a couple of associated city gates. In selected places the pilgrim is invited to climb up and take a gander, imagining himself a valiant defender of the town's virtue while pouring boiling oil or hurling stones down upon Moorish invaders. Or Christian invaders. Who did the pouring and who did the boiling depended, I suppose, on your point of view.

Mansilla was also a center for the preservation of the Leonese language. Between five thousand and fifty thousand people are thought to still speak the Leonese dialect, which gave me the impression that this was a wild guess and nobody really knows how many people are competent. UNESCO, in its *Atlas of Languages in Danger in the World*,[24] lists Leonese in the most at-risk category. The category's criteria are:

- Unofficial status
- Without legitimized significant use in the news media
- Low levels of proficiency and use
- Poor social prestige
- Not used as a medium of primary education
- Not used in official place names

Leonese separatist sentiments on display (Homo Charrus/Wikimedia CC BY-SA 4.0)

24. Moseley, *Atlas of Languages*.

Not many people understood me when I spoke Spanish, which was weird because I was certified as being 16 percent fluent according to Duolingo. Perhaps they only spoke Leonese. That must be the reason. No question about it.

After dinner we attended Mass at *Iglesia Santa Maria*, which—as usual—was only attended by the old women of the town. It seemed that the priest was just going through the motions, and the Mass finished after only thirty-five minutes.

After exchanging a few text messages with Allison and praying Compline, I signed off for the night, grateful for the gift of another day.

The *sello* of Albergue Gaia in Mansillas de Las Mulas

León

Was I terrified of the idea that I could experience another bout of kidney stones while on pilgrimage? Not terrified, exactly, but nervous enough that I had been drinking water on the trail like it was my job. When one's job is drinking water, an occupational hazard is frequent trips to the bathroom. Nobody wishes to awake from a dreamy slumber for this purpose, of course, but it is even less pleasant when frail-kidneyed pilgrims share sleeping accommodation with other trail mates. In Mansilla I got up twice during the night to use the bathroom. I was careful to avoid disturbing the dog accompanying one of the *peregrinos*, which slept where? In the bathroom. Naturally. Another helping of Camino strangeness.

The *hospitaleros* who owned Albergue Gaia put on a lovely breakfast for us, and because we had a relatively short walk into León we were very pleased to stick around for it. Bread, butter, strawberry jam, and real coffee with milk was very nice indeed, and all for whatever donation we cared to make. We really enjoyed this *albergue* and the people with whom we shared it. The lady of the house gave me a big hug as I was leaving. I will admit to growing a bit dewy-eyed at her kindness.

I guess we'll go this way

We walked for most of the twelve miles into León with Pam from New Hampshire. We had a fine chat about her career as a personal trainer, music educator, and cafe owner. We traded emails and would try to keep in touch. We also ran into Reinhard and Heide at various points along the walk and later in León's cathedral. They often hold hands while walking and are about the cutest couple of seventy-somethings you can imagine. Heide's leg was hurting her, but she was tough and soldiered on in good German fashion.

An hour after leaving Mansilla de las Mulas we strolled through Villarente. If one Googles this place, the little spinning icon in the middle of your screen will twirl for quite awhile before returning a few websites that provide little more than the weather and the local time. Still, our guidebook informed us that Villarente is noteworthy for having sponsored the Camino's very first ambulance service. While not up to modern standards, I am sure the donkey and cart that took sick pilgrims into medieval León was appreciated by those who needed it. One wonders if the bridge in Villarente the donkey cart-ambulance traversed actually spanned a waterway in those days. Today it is still a lovely bridge, and safely and conveniently conveys pilgrims over the grassy field in the town park.

Eventually we crested a hill and were rewarded with spectacular views of León in the valley below. The spires of the Gothic cathedral served as a kind of homing beacon guiding us toward the Old City. About three kilometers before entering León proper we came to the suburb of Puente

Castro. This place has a fascinating history as it once hosted a significant Jewish community. Archaeologists have uncovered grave markers that indicate the presence of a Jewish quarter that dates to the tenth century. Unfortunately for the good people of Puente Castro, in 1196 the kingdoms of Aragón and Castile decided they would gang up to teach neighboring León a lesson. Who were the big losers in this battle? The Jews. Their homes were destroyed and they were enslaved. Today the inscription on one of the unearthed tombstones serves as a reminder for all of us:[25]

> *Cientos the Saint may be blessed and absolved, take him in Your mercy and resurrect him to the life of the future world, amen.*

Pilgrims are frequently advised to skip the walk into (and out of) León by taking a taxi or bus, but we walked anyway. Richard Ford, writing in his *Handbook for Travellers in Spain* 170 years ago, claimed León as "decaying,"[26] but to be fair to that fine city, Ford uses some version of "decay" no fewer than fifty-six times to describe various Spanish communities. While the oldest parts of this ancient capital are nothing of the sort, the outskirts— both coming and going—are typical of a large, modern, gritty, industrial city. Still, we were prepared for a touch of the reality of the lived experience of León's people. This pilgrimage taught me to take what comes—good and less good—and be grateful for both.

It was easy to navigate León's old city to the Hotel Alfonso V where we checked in for a couple of nights to rest and see the sights. We were looking forward to both, remembering with fondness our leisure time in Burgos.

Being a lovely day and a Sunday to boot, the old part of León was hopping! We witnessed a festive parade of townsfolk playing instruments and carrying flags as we entered Plaza Santo Domingo where our hotel was located. This parade and quite a bit of associated hoopla was part of the festival dedicated to León's patron, San Froilán. This is a saint about whom I knew very little. A native of this part of Spain who lived in the ninth century, he was a holy child—the son of another saint—who transitioned from living as a hermit in the Cantabrian Mountains to serving as bishop of León for the last five years of his life. He did much good, and was greatly beloved by the people, who acclaimed him a saint immediately following his death. And in

---

25. JGuideEurope, "Puente Castro," https://jguideeurope.org/en/region/spain/castile-mancha-castile-leon/puente-castro-leon/.

26. Ford et al., *Handbook*, 659.

yet another adventure in *Languageland*, here is an excerpt from the *Wikipedia* entry through the sometimes-blurry lens of Google Translate:[27]

> *It is at this time when, according to legend, the episode of the wolf devouring its ass takes place. Contaminated by the saint, the fierce animal, as a meek lamb, he carries the saddlebags of the books that always accompanied San Froilán in his apostolic excursions.*

Anyone who can convince a wolf to devour its own ass is a saint in my book.

While the city was busy celebrating its patron saint when we visited, we were told that it was practically deserted compared to Holy Week— *Semana Santa*. During that week the various confraternities dust off their floats—handed down from generation to generation—and parade them through the streets in processions that can last twelve hours. I read the journal of a pilgrim who visited León during *Semana Santa*. He made it back to his *albergue* with two hours to spare before the doors would be locked at 10:00 p.m. All he had to do was get across the street that was serving as the venue for one of the city's many processions. He waited for the parade to go by, then waited some more. One hour went by, then forty-five minutes more. The procession lasted as far as the eye could see. Finally, thinking that he would have to sleep on a park bench if drastic measures were not employed, he jumped into the procession becoming, briefly, a pilgrim-participant. Moving stealthily from left to right he finally jumped out of line with only five minutes to spare. He fell asleep nearly immediately, but awoke at midnight to hear the procession still parading past the *albergue* window. This makes my hometown, Holland, Michigan's, Tulip Time parade seem like the minor leagues.

**Leónese confraternity in *capriote* processes during *Semana Santa*
(El Pantera/Wikimedia CC BY-SA 3.0)**

27. Wikipedia, s.v. "Froilán de León," last modified October 6, 2021, https://en.wikipedia.org/wiki/Felipe_de_Marichalar_y_Borb%C3%B3n.

León is also known for the legend of the one hundred virgins, in which the Moorish rulers of the Emirate of Cordoba demanded one hundred Christian virgins each year from the Asturian ruler Mauregato (aka Mauregatus the Usurper). The Christians ended the required tribute with a military victory at the mythical Battle of Clavijo, in which *Santiago Matamoros* was seen riding his white charger while mowing down Moorish fighters. The scholar Emily Francomano calls this story "historically apocryphal but ideologically accurate,"[28] as it reflects modern memory and popular interpretation of the Christian *reconquista* over the allegedly sexually libertine Moors.

The feckless Mauregatus the Usurper
(Manuel Iglesias y Domínguez/Wikimedia (public domain)

León is named for the Roman legion that was stationed there. It was founded in the first century BC by the Roman legion *Legio VI Victrix*, which served under Caesar Augustus during the Cantabrian Wars (29–19 BC), the final stage of the Roman conquest of Hispania. In the year AD 74, the *Legio VII Gemina*—recruited from the Hispanics by the Spanish Roman general, Galba, in AD 69—settled in a permanent military camp that was the origin of the city. Its modern name, León, is derived from the city's Latin name *Legio*.[29] In 1188, the city hosted the first parliament in

28. Francomano, "Legend," 9.

29. Wikipedia, s.v. "List of Roman Legions," last modified February 28, 2022, https://en.wikipedia.org/wiki/List_of_Roman_legions.

European history under the reign of Alfonso IX, thus earning it the reputation as the cradle of parliamentarism. The *Decreta of León* serves as the first written record of this form of government, and was included in the *Memory of the World* register by UNESCO in 2013.[30]

After showers, laundry, and a wee nap we set out for the León Cathedral which was just a few blocks away. This church was a wonder of early Gothic architecture with stained glass of unbelievable abundance and beauty. The ceilings seemed to soar to the heavens. It was simply gorgeous. The art critic Edwin Mullins has this to say about this treasure:

> It is not simply that León Cathedral has the best stained glass in Spain—which it does: to enter the chill, twilit interior of this place and look around in the gloom until, by chance, the sun chooses that moment to come out is, I felt, to comprehend something of the hold which the Christian faith has been able to retain over so many people and for so long . . . I was astonished, and moved. God, it seemed, had been invented by the glassmaker's art.[31]

The beauty of León Cathedral, it seems, was enough to impart a sense of the numinous on even the most hardened atheist.

The sun that pours through León Cathedral's soaring windows fills the space with characteristically Spanish light (Txo/Wikimedia CC BY-SA 3.0)

30. UN Educational, Scientific and Cultural Organization, "Memory of the World."
31. Mullins, *Pilgrimage to Santiago*, 186.

We had our pilgrim passports stamped at the cathedral's museum and spent considerable time strolling through the massive church admiring its many treasures. The impression that such a place as this must have made on the medieval mind is hard to underestimate. Churches of this size and grandeur took decades—even generations—to build. The fortunes of entire families were linked to the economies that such churches generated. If my jaw dropped when seeing such a place, what was the reaction of a common thirteenth-century peasant who lived with his entire family in one dark, smoky room?

Gaudí sits in front of his *Casa Botines* while taking none of my advice

After a stroll through the supermarket we headed back to the room for a snack and a snooze. Our stomachs stirred us from our naps and we went in search of dinner. It was still early by Spanish standards, but we were hoping to find a place that would satisfy Joe's longing for a hamburger. Before long we stumbled upon a bar advertising *hamburguesas completas* and were in business. Inside the bar we ran into the three Minnesotans with whom we walked out of Burgos. They were footsore with blisters and tendinitis, which helped me count my blessings for how well my body was holding up. They were lovely people, and we enjoyed a good chat. After we finished eating, a threesome seated behind us asked if we were walking the

Camino. Joe—the seventy-something dad—was doing his third Camino, and his son and daughter-in-law had joined him in León to walk the rest of the way to Santiago de Compostela. They were from Milwaukee, and a light-hearted Michigan versus Wisconsin football back-and-forth ensued. Joe warned us of a big music festival that would take place in Santiago de Compostela about the time we were scheduled to arrive. This intelligence encouraged us to book accommodation in advance so we had a place to sleep. We were grateful for the advice, and decided we would at least book a room for the night before our flight home. I admit to feeling some trepidation at busier Camino traffic once we hit the home stretch that might cause anxiety about room in the *albergues*. We decided that we would take it a day at a time, booking ahead as we thought necessary based on our experience as it comes.

After a quick look at the now-illuminated cathedral, we headed back to the hotel for a luxurious night of rest with laundered sheets, fluffy towels, no snoring, and no alarm clock. The cathedral lit from dozens of outdoor lights was almost as impressive as the natural light that flooded the massive windows during our walk around earlier in the day.

A day off provides a good opportunity to dedicate some time to thinking about how this pilgrimage was benefitting me in a spiritual sense. I was increasingly mindful of Pope Benedict XVI's perspective:[32]

> To go on pilgrimage is not simply to visit a place to admire its trea-
> sures of nature, art or history. To go on pilgrimage really means to
> step out of ourselves in order to encounter God where he has revealed
> himself, where his grace has shone with particular splendour and
> produced rich fruits of conversion and holiness among those who
> believe.

Before my head hit the pillow I called home to talk with Carol for the first time in a week. What a special treat this was for me. We did not discuss anything earthshaking. There was no big news to share. But the sound of our voices floating across the internet and connecting in heartspace was the nourishment my soul needed for the next part of the pilgrimage. After offering a prayer for my old friend, Bob Moss—who was worried about a recent cancer diagnosis—I called it a day, and looked forward to a night of *albergue*-free slumber.

---

32. Kosloski, "Here's Why."

The stamp of the León Cathedral

Our Zero Day

After a terrific night of uninterrupted sleep, we awoke at 8:30 in a refreshed state. And hungry! It did not take long to dig into our grocery store breakfast.

After showering (another day-off luxury, a morning shower) we strolled over to the Basilica of San Isidore. This has been a church of particular importance since medieval times. In 1168 Ferdinand II, king of Castile, decreed that the pilgrim road through León should be rerouted past the basilica's front door so pilgrims could visit his father's (Ferdinand I) burial place along with that of St. Isidore, who, rather improbably, is the modern—day patron saint of the Internet.[33] A new gate to the city was constructed to facilitate this royally mandated route change.[34] The church is terrific as most have been in Spain, and after a *cafe con leche* we decide to spend five euros to tour the museum and cloisters. Our English-speaking tour guide provided an excellent description of the many treasures housed there. A very well spent five euros.

We wandered around a much quieter León for awhile, then went back to the hotel where we made a picnic of grocery store leftovers. Naps for everyone after that. We were supposed to be resting, after all. It was our day off. And we were very tired. And needed our sleep. Don't judge us.

33. Telegraph reporters, "Patron Saint."
34. Webb, *Medieval European Pilgrimage*, 36.

Joe and I love a grocery store lunch

We attended the 7:00 p.m. pilgrim Mass at San Isidore and received a heartfelt pilgrim blessing afterward. The day's prayer intentions were centered on the gratitude I felt for some of my Hope College colleagues, including Jared Ortiz and Jeff Tyler. They were good friends to me, and I was grateful for all they had done to support me, especially in recent months.

The Pantheon below the Basilica of St. Isidore
(Jaume/Wikimedia CC0 1.0) *Public Domain Dedication*

Following Mass we stopped at a restaurant in the plaza outside the church for dinner. We jokingly commented that it was about time for Brock and Sue to show up. Five minutes later they turned the corner and we all had a good laugh. They joined us for dinner and we had a lovely time.

Villar de Mazarife was the destination for the next day. But first, one more night in comfortable circumstances.

The *sello* of the *Basilica de San Isidoro* in León

The Ending

Out of the Gritty City

T HE reality of our pilgrimage came rushing back as the alarm woke us at 6:00 in our comfortable beds in Hotel Alfonso V. We ate the last of our grocery store Napoleons and yogurt and headed out onto the quiet streets of León in search of the yellow arrows that would guide us to Santiago de Compostela.

It can be tricky exiting a big city in the dark, and we were warned that the walk out of León required extra care. I was glad for Joe's extra set of eyes. Between the two of us we avoided any wrong turns.

Navigating our exit from León in the dark past the Parador *Hostal de San Marcos*
(m.dolores paderne sanchez/Wikimedia CC BY-SA 3.0)

As the sky brightened we said goodbye to the skyline of León and hello to the *Basílica de la Virgen del Camino*. This monument serves as the pilgrim's last look at suburban León, for as soon as we crossed the street we were back out into the countryside. The basilica was notable as the first modern church we encountered since our arrival in Spain. Constructed in 1961, the facade was decorated with the statues of twelve apostles surrounding Jesus. This church was located in the place where the Virgin Mary appeared to a shepherd in 1505. The local bishop, desiring proof of the purported visitation, was finally convinced when the shepherd—on the instructions of the Virgin—shot a stone from his slingshot to the place where she desired the church to be built. The stone—transformed into a boulder in mid-flight—won the bishop over.

La Basílica de la Virgen del Camino

The rural precincts we encountered after we left the León's suburban outskirts were described in Joe's guidebook as "moorland" but reminded me of Leelanau County, Michigan, with gently rolling hills and farm fields. The Irago Range of the Cantabrian Mountains stared us in the face most of the day, much as the Rockies do when driving toward Denver. We would climb those things in a couple of days.

The day's walk was dedicated to Trygve Johnson, whose friendship I appreciated very much. I prayed for him, and gave thanks for his faithful presence in my life. The events of the previous six months were hard on him, and I prayed that he could get back to a place where he could flourish again.

We had intentions of spending the night in Villar de Mazarife—a walk of about fourteen miles from León. But when we arrived around 11:45 it seemed too early to quit, so we decided to eat lunch and push on to Villa-vante—another ten kilometers. We called ahead and booked beds in the Albergue Santa Lucia to make sure we could be assured of having a place to sleep. The decision to push on was a good one. Villar de Mazarife was described by our guidebook as "a friendly pilgrim town," and perhaps it was. Its 391 people were no doubt awash in virtue. Still, if one checks TripAdvisor's list of top ten things to do in this friendly place, you are provided with advice to get in your car and drive somewhere else. We would take our chances in Villavante.

Santiago Peregrino, all alone in Villar de Mazarife

As we finished lunch two young women who were part of our pilgrim bubble since leaving France strolled into the plaza. Aleah was from the Pacific Northwest and Patricia was an Aussie who was on leave from her job as an EMT in England. We walked together the last six miles into Villavante, which made our total mileage for the day a bone-wearying 19.7 miles. It was fun passing the time and enduring the somewhat dull landscapes by taking turns singing songs, including Patricia's rendition of her homeland's unofficial national anthem, *Waltzing Matilda*.

We were glad to see the barns, sheds, and other agricultural buildings that constitute Villavante come into view. The *albergue* was nice. Aleah and Patricia pushed on the extra three kilometers to Hospital de Orbigo.

Perhaps we would run into them the next day. Or maybe the day after that. Or perhaps never again. Such is the pilgrim way.

Our ablutions completed, we sat outside the *albergue* with Sinta and Frank from Pittsburgh. They have walked various sections of the Camino, and were traveling the section between Lograño and Ponferrada that year. We were also pleased to see Mike and Margie from Australia again. We met this couple some days before and had crossed paths from time to time as our pilgrim bubble expanded and contracted according to some law of nature I didn't understand. They preferred to stay in *albergues* that offered the option of a private room, which included the Albergue Santa Lucía. I have a sneaking suspicion that if I was ever lucky enough to coax Carol onto the Camino it would be on the basis of private sleeping quarters. The love of my life is not an *albergue* gal, methinks.

While chatting with a fellow pilgrim in the *albergue's* lobby I was surprised to hear the cry of a small child. Babies are not unknown along the Camino—we spent the night with one in Roncesvalles. And in the bigger cities we saw mothers with their children strolling the plazas under the warming sun. But children were rare enough that one noticed them when they crossed the Camino's path. Not crazy, just unusual. What was surprising in that moment was when I turned to admire the source of this call and spotted instead a parrot mimicking the cry of a human child. Or perhaps it was a macaw. In any case, it was a domesticated tropical bird perched atop its cage. This was charming until it occurred to me that Polly the Parrot / Molly the Macaw might maintain his (*Her*? Who knows?) caterwauling past the "lights-out" hour. I prayed to God Almighty and all of the saints that this cup might pass us by.

Small bird. Big mouth.

150

The bunk room was relatively quiet, but I still had a hard time sleeping soundly. I was typically either too warm or too cold. "Just right" did not seem to exist in *albergue* living. Again, I was getting the sleep I needed (just not the sleep I wanted), and I needed to work on a spirit of gratitude for that.

Our Albergue Santa Lucía stamp

Two Pilgrims Disagree

I'm not sure how one quiets a parrot, macaw, or any other species of bird. But I am very grateful to the *hospitalero* who did. Polly/Molly did not let out a peep in the night.

The morning's walk was lovely. The absolute flat of the *meseta* was gradually changing to rolling hills, with the Cantabrian Mountains in the foreground. We walked for quite awhile with Mike, Margie, and three of their Aussie countrymen. Jokesters and cutups! It made for fun walking. I wish we had spent more time on the trail with these guys.

The long medieval bridge in Hospital de Orbigo was really something. We stopped for a *cafe con leche, tortilla patata,* and toast at the far end of the bridge—a good way to fuel us for the next few hours.

The long bridge in Hospital de Orbigo at sunrise

The bridge has an interesting history. In the Holy Year of 1434 the Leonese knight Suero de Quiñones staged a chivalric *passo honoroso* at the bridge. He and ten of his best knightly buddies set up camp next to the bridge and challenged all comers to a joust as payment for crossing. The bridge was a vital artery of pilgrimage and commerce, and Suero thought he would have no problem at all in defeating at least three hundred challengers. He and the fellas did not do badly, but after tallying 166 victories he declared victory, confident that honor had been satisfied as he tried to avoid further wear and tear on his team and himself.[1]

We passed an interesting place a few kilometers before Astorga. *Casa de los Dioses* is a kind of rest stop for pilgrims, with shady sitting places, a hammock, and a variety of fruit and snacks. The proprietor, David, lives in the shack/shed/house out back and gives it all away for free and is known to be quite a character. Joe and I both enjoyed a delicious pear. I left a euro in the box to help keep the operation going.

Take what you want, leave what you can at *Casa de Los Dioses*
(Kolossus/Wikimedia CC BY-SA 3.0)

Joe and I had been the best of partners. The Spirit that brought us together so many months before had infused our relationship so richly throughout our summertime training, trip planning, and through hundreds of miles of walking in Spain. But even good friends have their moments, and we had one approaching Astorga. And it was my fault. Our decision to walk an additional ten kilometers the day before was a good one. It gave us the chance to enjoy the company of Aleah and Patricia. It helped us use the

1. Evans, *Critical Annotated Edition*, 5.

early part of the afternoon for walking. It reconnected us with Mike and Margie and their friends. But the downside of that decision was that the stretch between Villavante and Astorga was shortened considerably—to only thirteen miles, which we could now walk in our sleep. This might not have been a big deal—heck, it might have even been a welcome development—if the weather was inclement. If the sun was burning us to cinders or the rain was forcing us to pull our feet from sucking mud with each step, we might have happily given away everything we owned to see the spires of Astorga's cathedral rising before us. But the day was beautiful. A perfect day for walking. A pilgrim's dream. And since it was only noon, and since I was starting to feel the tug of Santiago de Compostela the closer we got to Galicia, and because I'm prone to occasional sinful moodiness, I wanted to keep walking straight through Astorga and put more miles behind us. Joe wanted to stop and see the sights. We had faced this decision near the end of other days on the Camino and always come to an amicable decision. I do not know what my problem was on this particular day, but I grew grumpy at the idea of quitting so early. Perhaps I was losing the spirit of "it's the journey, not the destination" now that we were getting closer to the destination. I gave into Joe's preference, but I was a bit of a sullen jerk about it. I would do it differently if given the chance.

A pilgrim in bronze atop the hill before Astorga

Joe's instincts to stop in Astorga were spot-on, and I was, well, a big dummy. Astorga was a terrific place to spend time, and looking back on it, I realize now that missing Astorga would have impoverished our pilgrimage experience. The *albergue* we chose, *Albergue de Peregrinos Siervas de María*, had a wonderful, welcoming spirit. I guess it infected me, for after going through our usual *albergue* arrival routine I felt more centered and ready to explore this interesting community.

By now, Dear Reader, you know that Joe and I enjoy strolling through a grocery store looking for novel ways to satisfy our various cravings. Astorga was no exception. We spotted a "Dia" *supermercado* in the plaza where we bought *empanadas carnes* and Cokes for lunch. I can now check grocery store *empanadas* off my list as comestibles that qualify as "food." They tasted like a Hot Pocket filled with dog food. Yuck.

After lunch we strolled over to the cathedral for a look around. The cathedral was a bit severe in appearance. It lacked the Gothic "wow-factor" of the Burgos cathedral and the soaring airiness of its León cousin. Two-thirds of the church was constructed of a reddish stone while the other third seemed decidedly lighter in color. It was almost as if the builders ran out of one kind of stone and had to switch to another kind. It was still a fantastic place—one we were lucky to be able to visit.

"Pass me a dark stone." "Sorry, we're fresh out."

A funny thing happened while Joe and I strolled through the cathedral marveling at its many treasures,[2] including the *retablo* of St. Michael, and the large high altar. There was a fellow scurrying around preparing the massive sanctuary for an upcoming feast day or similar important event. He lassoed Joe and—without a syllable of English—dazzled him with a bit of sign language and before you know it Joe was helping him carry a near-life size statue of the Blessed Mother up to a place of prominence near the altar. Did the priceless sculpture tilt a bit as Assistant Sacristan Joe lifted the Virgin onto her platform? Maybe just a bit, but soon she was suitably positioned and I could breathe easy again.

Don't worry. It was only an ancient, priceless, irreplaceable object of sacred sculpture that this guy asked Joe the Passing Stranger to move.

The cathedral dates from ancient times. The old Romanesque structure was destroyed in 1265. Construction began in earnest on the present church in 1471, and is a mixture of Baroque, Gothic, Classical, and Renaissance styles. Both St. James and St. Paul are, by tradition, reputed to have preached in Astorga. St. Francis of Assisi visited Astorga while on pilgrimage to Santiago.

After spending a couple of hours and getting Mary straightened out we walked next door to take in the Episcopal Palace. Designed by Gaudí and built in the early twentieth century, this building was built to serve as

---

2. Many of which are catalogued in the Metropolitan Museum of Art's *The Art of Medieval Spain: A.D. 500–1200*, 175–84.

the bishop's residence. It was appropriated by the *Falange* (the sole legal political party during the Franco years) at the beginning of the Spanish Civil War. Eventually the presiding bishop recognized that the building was far too grand to serve as his home, and he wisely had it repurposed as the *Museo de los Caminos*, dedicated to the Way of St. James.

The Gaudi-designed Episcopal Palace in Astorga gives off a Hogwarts vibe (Wikimedia CC0 1.0 Public Domain Dedication)

Before dinner we took part in a prayer service provided by the *albergue* volunteers. It was a lovely, intimate service conducted in four languages—Spanish, English, French, and German. Various Camino-themed scriptures were read, prayers were offered, and the facilitator—who was one of the staff that checked us in when we arrived earlier in the day—provided a short reflection. My prayers were offered for Fr. Charlie Brown in gratitude for his friendship, pastoral care, ministry, and all-around goodness. I love that guy. The prayer service was a really nice way to cap off the day.

I missed my family terribly. I suspected that an element of my grumpiness earlier in the day was occasioned by the crazy idea that if I could only walk a bit farther I'd be that much closer to seeing them again. This was irrational, of course, since our return tickets were already set for October 21—a mere two weeks from then. Still, Carol said that she would get a puppy if I did not return soon. I needed to get home and head that idea off at the pass—and quickly.

The Friends of the Camino and the Cathedral stamped our pilgrim passports in Astorga

Up

Among my evening routines before falling asleep was sending a note home to the family. These missives usually include photos and thoughts that banged around in my head for any particular day of walking. The Wi-Fi in our Astorga *albergue* was very spotty, so I could not send my journal entry that night as I wanted to. Still, a video of Kennedy kicking and chatting away made it through, and fortified me for the day's walk.

We said goodbye to Astorga as we walked its darkened streets, past the cathedral and Gaudí's episcopal palace, and out into the countryside. I was very glad we spent the time we did in Astorga, and regretted my kvetchiness at wanting to walk farther the day before. Except for the *empanadas*, Astorga was cool.

The day's walk was a slow, gradual climb from the Bierzo valley up into the Cantabrians. The Bierzo region—like just about every place through which we walked—had an interesting history and several distinctive cultural peculiarities. It was surrounded by mountains on three sides, which has rendered it a bit isolated. Spanish is the official language, but Leonese and the *gallego* spoken in Galicia began to mix in this place. Since I have already established that my fluency in Leonese was far below that of my proficiency in Spanish, this would make for an interesting couple of days. That neck of the woods was also home to a few dozen villages—principally centered around Astorga—that reflected the cultural influences of the Maragato people. These folks are thought to be the last remnants of the Berber Moors who emigrated to (or *invaded* depending on your point of view) the Iberian Peninsula in the eighth century. There are thought to be approximately four thousand living Maragatos, who by tradition have been muleteers, and in practice have been a marginalized minority group in Spain.[3] My guidebook informed me that the Bierzo valley was home to

3. Wilkinson, "Spain's 'Damned' Maragatos."

holly, birch, and maple trees, which after the nearly treeless *meseta* sounded delightful. Deer could evidently be found there. Perhaps we'd see one, which would be lovely. The wild boar, badgers, and wolves that call Bierzo home could stay away, thank you very much.

Maragatos in traditional costume (Rodelar, CC BY—SA 3.0, via Wikimedia Commons)

The first little town we came to after leaving Astorga was Valdeviejas, population 156. This town's claim to fame is its small church, *La Ermita del Ecce Homo*. The townsfolk celebrate the Festival of Ecce Homo annually on May 6. The people process through the town with statues of Jesus Christ and the Virgin Mary. The procession continues through the various fields where blessings are offered for the crops, including—rather improbably— the humble chickpea. I appreciate this regard for the chickpea, for soups and stews made from this legume are terrifically tasty.[4]

We walked most of the day with Brock and Sue, who we ran into when we stopped for coffee in the delightfully named village of El Ganso ("The Goose"). The town has an *albergue*, and when it is half full, the population of the village doubles. The cafe we chose (well, we did not actually *choose* it, as it was the only one on offer) was called *Meson COWBOY* and was decorated in the style of the American Old West. Elvis was playing on the radio. As we were sipping our drinks I thought to myself, "Here I am having a drink in Spain with South Africans residing in Australia in a bar designed to make me think I'm in a John Wayne movie while listening to Elvis." *Alice in Wonderland* came to mind.

4. "Valdeviejas Celebra," Astorga Redacción, May 3, 2018.

We enjoyed a coffee with Brock and Sue in this interesting cafe in El Ganso

Most of the guidebooks recommend stopping at Rabinal del Camino, but we decided to just make a quick pit stop there, change socks, have a Coke, and push on another three miles to Foncebadón. Though our decision to push past Rabinal made our walk from Astorga just over sixteen miles—with the last three steeply uphill on a very rocky path—it provided a down payment on the next day's hike, which was likely to be a bit challenging anyway.

A poem I wrote a few years prior to our pilgrimage came to mind as we entered the crumbling precincts of Foncebadón while leaning forward on tired legs, *The Shady Place*:

I walk down the path where it bends
In the deepening woods. Dew-glistened ferns
Sway gently in the breeze. Singing their
Forest song. And my thoughts are troubled
By doubts. About the journey. And the path
I've chosen. It's dark ahead.
Dim visions of unknown steps.
What does this trek want from me? What
Do I need from it? The track narrows and grows rocky
As I climb higher. My eyes see the ground
Only. The sky is for the sure-footed.
The day grows hot. My tongue searches for water
Like a desert plant wants moisture.
A million steps and the dust of the path
Are my constant companions.

But there—ahead—clinging to the mountainside
A tree. Shading the way. A respite
For my soul. Deep roots carving
A grip in the living stone.
Rain and hail and gale have tried
To have their way. But the sentinel
Endures. Spreading branch and leaf.
In its cool embrace I find shelter. Encouragement
In living form.

And strength for the way ahead.

El Ganso fixer-upper

We chuffed into Foncebadón on fumes and scanned the grim surroundings for the least decrepit *albergue* on offer. This place was all but abandoned as a population center or Camino way station, but in recent years had experienced a modest renaissance. The buildings were principally constructed of stone, though it must be observed that most of the buildings were, in fact, former buildings. Our guidebook described the village as "rustic" and characterized by a "timeless atmosphere." Imagine a Spanish ghost town framed as a Wild West movie set. Gratefully, we encountered no wild dogs as actor Shirley McLain did when she walked the Camino. Or ghosts, though the village did feel a bit haunted.

We noticed that the Camino was getting busier, with most of the added traffic coming from people who were not carrying packs, and who appeared to be supported by tour companies. My initial reaction to this was to be upset that these imposters were imposing on my pilgrimage. But then I stepped back from that uncharitable point of view and realized that everyone makes their pilgrimage in their own manner, and I should not judge. I would need to be more patient as I shared the Camino with more people. This "class difference" between pilgrims was a problem for medieval *peregrini* as well. Everyday folk making the pilgrimage to Jerusalem would normally seek hospitality at the Hospital of St. John. The fat cats, on the other hand, would lodge in style with the Franciscans on Mount Sion. In a sermon (*Veneranda Dies*) contained in the first volume of the *Codex Calixtinus*, one preacher railed against the spiritual inequity related to the financial differences between common and high-born pilgrims, decrying those who enter the holy precincts on horseback. These "thieves and robbers" have, he claims, "abandoned the way of specific apostolic poverty and chosen instead the path of damnation."[5] Well. Joe and I would strive for a more charitable point of view.

Our *albergue*—Roger de Lauria—was a former convent. Our bunk room was shared with Brock and Sue, Frank and Sinda (from Pittsburgh, who we met in Villavante a couple of days previous), and Sylvia—a German we'd seen from time to time for a few weeks.

The little toe on my left foot gave me some trouble that day, and I wondered if it might nag me for awhile longer. It felt like I bruised the soft flesh under the nail, which meant I would probably lose the nail eventually. Oh well, it would fit in nicely with the rest of the collection.

My sore foot didn't seem that bad compared to this guy

5. Sumption, *Pilgrimage*, 208.

Within a couple of kilometers after Foncebadón we would encounter the *Cruz de Ferro*. Joe wanted some private time there so he walked ahead that afternoon and would double back to the *albergue* in time for dinner. It would be dark-ish in the morning when I saw it for the first time. I hoped to have my visit there at sunrise. The *Cruz de Ferro* (Iron Cross) sits atop a hill of stones deposited on a windswept plain at the highest point of the Camino. It is a "thin" place imbued with enchanted meaning since pre-Christian times. A holy hermit—Gaucelmo—repurposed it as a place of Christian devotion. For centuries pilgrims to St. James have placed a stone from their home at the foot of the cross as a symbolic gesture representing the laying down of their burdens, sins, and spiritual anxieties. I had been carrying my own stone since April, and I was very much looking forward to laying it down once and for all at *Cruz de Ferro*. I watched a video diary of a pilgrim who wept with terrific emotion when arriving at *Cruz de Ferro*. The psychic weight seemed to drain away with his tears as he committed to live a more virtuous life. I knew how he felt, and wondered if my encounter with this holy site would have a similar effect on me.

The walk to Foncebadón was dedicated to Fr. Bill VanderWerff. I was grateful for the cheerful nature of his ministry, and hoped God would bless him richly as he carried the gospel to all those to whom he ministered.

We enjoyed the pilgrim dinner prepared by the *hospitaleros*. I enjoyed a spicy garlic soup, fish and chips (French fries, always French fries—every day), and ice cream. Joe and I were joined by Sue and Brock, Ernest from Pretoria, Sylvia from Cologne, and Don from Phoenix. The conversation was enjoyable and light-hearted.

The staple food of pilgrimage
(Tom Head from Washington, DC, CC BY 2.0, via Wikimedia Commons)

I finished my day—as usual—by thanking God for the many blessings he has bestowed on me, including the gift of being able to take time away to walk the Camino while opening myself to the Holy Spirit and His healing presence. As I reflected I could confess to an increasing desire—something akin to a physical ache—to be reunited with my family. My emotions were muddled—influenced by both thankfulness for the Camino and a desire to reach its end and return home.

Our pilgrim passport stamp from Foncebadón

Burdened No More

I enjoyed a decent night of sleep, extended by a later-than-usual alarm to allow us to visit *Cruz de Ferro* in the light of breaking dawn. We lingered a bit in the *albergue* and enjoyed a breakfast of coffee (*con leche*, naturally) and toast with margarine and jam with Frank and Sinda. They would fly home after reaching Ponferrada later in the day.

The walk to *Cruz de Ferro* from Foncebadón took only about thirty minutes of gentle uphill walking in a comfortable, cool mountain climate. Once there, I offered a prayer for my family and friends, for those people I know who are sick or dying, and finally for God's help in continuing to cleanse my heart (and even my memory) of anger and bitterness. Then I reverently placed the stone I had carried since April at the foot of the cross. It was the high point of the pilgrimage for me. I could feel my spirit beginning to heal, and for this I was so very grateful. I had worried for many months that the illness described by St. Thomas More (1478–1535) might never find a cure in my lifetime:

This deadly cancer of anger from which so much harm grows: It makes us unlike ourselves, makes us like timber wolves or furies from hell, drives us forth headlong upon the points of swords, makes us blindly run forth after other men's destruction as we hasten toward our own ruin.[6]

My pilgrimage to date—especially that day's arrival at *Cruz de Ferro*—was giving me hope, even confidence, that I might achieve a level of equanimity and consolation. I hoped so.

I laid down my stone—and my anger—at the *Cruz de Ferro*.

Joe and I loitered awhile at *Cruz de Ferro* to watch the sunrise warm the Irago Mountains over which we were walking. It was a beautiful experience, and one enjoyed by the other pilgrims gathered at this sacred site.

Not too long after we left *Cruz de Ferro* we came to one of the strangest places on the road to Santiago. Manjarín was a shepherd's hut / sheep pen / garage sale-pile-of-junk that served as a crude, cold-water *albergue*. The *hospitaletero* of this swapsale junkyard was Tómas, a wizened recluse who fashioned himself as the last Grand Master of the Knights Templar. Though his health has forced him to live for a time in more modern circumstances down in the valley, Tómas could still be found in Manjarín chatting to pilgrims and providing them with information on the Templars. He was, I suppose, a man in the spirit of the early medieval hermits who lived along the road and were responsible for helping make the Camino a safe place for tired, sore, hungry pilgrims in need of human succor.

6. Quoted at http://www.catholicstoreroom.com/2017/01/08/anger-makes-us/.

Pilgrims approach the Manjarín kingdom of Tomás, the last Grand Master of the
Knights Templar (Marathoni62 at German Wikipedia, Public domain, via Wikimedia
Commons)

The walk over the Irago Mountains was breathtakingly beautiful. It
was also very challenging. We walked seventeen miles between Foncebadón
and Ponferrada, and much of it was steeply downhill over rough, rocky
paths. I spent much of the time looking down, though I was careful to look
up from time to time to take in the views.

The Irago Mountains are the highest point of the Camino Frances

We could see our destination—Ponferrada—from early in the day after we summited the mountain. It took us the whole day to arrive, reminding me once again of the importance of patience, and moving step-by-step toward a valued goal. In some ways, the walk that day felt like a kind of penance. Physically demanding, it reminded me that in earlier times penance for sins was a common motivation for pilgrims.[7] The form of the Sacrament of Reconciliation we know today has evolved substantially over the last two millennia. In the early church penitents would confess their sins publicly before the assembled congregation of worshipers before the Liturgy of the Eucharist. The Council of Nicaea in 325 mentions that penitents should be assigned to one of four stations during Mass. *Weepers*—the lowest stage—would be assigned to stand outside the church door while wailing and groaning. *Hearers* stood in the vestibule, but were sent out of the church before the Eucharist. *Kneelers*—dressed in sackcloth and covered in ash—were positioned at the back of the congregation, and remained kneeling when everyone else stood. *Co-standers* mingled with the congregation, but could not receive communion. And in those days penance was a "one-and-done" deal. The sinner was forgiven once, and only once, which is why many rolled the dice and hoped to confess their sins only on their deathbeds.

A codified system of penances for various sins eventually developed—first in Ireland and then in other European locations. These so-called "penitentials" were used—first by bishops and later by priests—to standardize the penance assigned to those desiring absolution from sin. One of the penances for grave sin was exile from the community. This took on the form of pilgrimage and could be permanent or temporary. The *Milan Penitential* specified, for example, that a priest found to be "intimate with a spiritual daughter" (someone he baptized or served as confessor) should go on pilgrimage for twelve years and be confined to a monastery when he returned. The *Penitential of Cummean* prescribed that monks who committed murder after taking a "vow of perfection" would be subject to "perpetual pilgrimage." Clerics and laypersons who committed the same sin would typically receive different penances as a reflection of their different expectations for holiness. A dejected monk, for example, was subject to temporary exile (pilgrimage) to another monastery where he would subsist on bread and water "until he can be joyful" again. Yikes. But not to worry. If one was well-off, he could simply pay a fine or hire a substitute to make

7. McNeill and Gamer, *Medieval Handbooks*, 141.

pilgrimage in his stead and through this means have his sanctity restored.[8] One of the systems of penances developed by St. Patrick pricks the modern conscience with its seeming lack of fairness. Under his system, one who stole from a church would be subject to one of three penances to be determined by drawing lots: his hand or foot would be cut off, or he would be imprisoned and forced to make restitution, or he would be forced to make a pilgrimage, restore double the value of what he stole, and after returning to the community become a monk. Dark Ages *Wheel of Fortune*.

By the medieval period priests and bishops were given some latitude to forgo the standard penances described by the penitentials based on circumstances. The twelfth-century *Penitential of Bartholomew Iscanus* was one such guide. Bartholomew—a contemporary of both King Henry II and Thomas Becket—was willing to forego some of the more common penances depending on the circumstances. It might not be necessary for the salvation of the soul in every occasion to groan, submit to "corporal blows," or undergo periods of enforced silence. Bartholomew goes so far as to relax the requirement of pilgrimage, which in those days could take on the form of banishment. When you went to confession you hoped that the priest—if he could read—had read Bartholomew, and was in a good mood.

The path was busy, but seemed to empty a bit after we left Molinaseca following a quick lunch and sock-changing break. It could be that many pilgrims stopped for the night in Molinaseca. The popular Brierley guidebook lists that place as the end of a stage. Molinaseca also seemed like a cool place to stay. But we pushed on to Ponferrada, which was also an interesting place. The walk into Ponferrada seemed endless. Once we entered the suburbs we may have strayed a bit from the prescribed path. One minute we were on a sidewalk and the next minute we were following a vague, rather unofficial-looking yellow arrow into an alley that led to the backside of a string of industrial buildings and warehouses. We followed our internal compasses for awhile, confident that we were walking toward the city center. Eventually we found ourselves at the bottom of a brush-filled valley with a crummy-looking stream off to our left with the city on our right on top of a sizable slope. There were no yellow arrows anywhere. Ditto for scallop shells. We trudged up the hill with rather creative curses muttered under our breath wondering when the &%$#?! we were going to

8. A pilgrimage to Santiago de Compostela assigned by a priest could be avoided by paying a fine of twelve livres—the fourteenth-century equivalent of two knight's horses or two gold rings with rubies. Freeman, *Holy Bones*, 105.

finally arrive. And at the top of the hill our intrepid wayfinding skills were rewarded by the sight of the *Albergue San Nicolàs de Flüe*. Finally, and not a minute too soon.

We checked into the *albergue*, which was operated by members of a Swiss confraternity. One of the *hospitaleros* was sitting in the courtyard with a first aid kit attending to the wreckage of various pilgrims' damaged feet. The hostel seemed very nice. Joe and I bunked with two young men from Israel—the first Israelis we had met on the Camino.

After showering and laundry, Joe, Sue, Brock, and I toured the Templar Castle. The castle was originally a *castro* (the Latin is *castrum*, meaning military camp) during Roman times. In 1178 the king of León gave the site to the Templars for the purpose of protecting the road to Santiago. The Templars gradually built it up over the next hundred years into the form it now has. Unfortunately for the Templars, their days were quickly coming to an ignominious end, so they did not occupy the castle for all that long. The castle was a great way to kill a couple of hours. It had an impressive library of medieval texts, including an original of the *Codex Calixtinus*.

Ponferrada's basilica framed by a dark sky

Touring a castle is hungry, exhausting work. After we grew weary of the views from the various crenellations and parapets, we joined Brock and Sue in the plaza near the basilica for a delightful dinner under a clear evening sky. This was a nice way to wrap up our afternoon in Ponferrada, which, by the way, means "iron bridge."

The Templar knight guards his castle—and keeps the Camino safe for pilgrims

The next day we would head for Villafranca Del Bierzo, which was about fifteen miles away and a looked to be a much gentler walk than the walk to Ponferrada. My legs were looking forward to a little less up and down.

Sello of the *Albergue San Nicolàs de Flüe*

In the Valley

I had a good sleep in the *Albergue San Nicolàs de Flüe* (the patron saint of Switzerland). Though it was a large *refugio*, the rooms accommodate only four pilgrims, and Joe and I arrived early enough to get the lower bunks. The two Israeli young men who shared our room were just out of the army. They were pleasant but kept mostly to themselves. It would have been interesting to know more of their stories.

San Nicolàs de Flüe, patron saint of the Swiss people, pray for us!

We strolled out of Ponferrada in the dark, passing by the Templar castle and the basilica. We took sad note of the bad problem this otherwise lovely city had with graffiti. The city's buildings seemed to be held upright by the quantity of spray paint festooning their walls. It was everywhere. And it was by and large vandalism posing as art and opinion. Very little of the Ponferrada graffiti had the charm or aesthetic interest of much of the Camino graffiti we had seen thus far on our journey. So saith the grumpy old man as he tottered westward.

Seventeen kilometers after leaving Ponferrada we came to the village of Cacabelos. There was not much to the town, though it provided another example of Spain's regionalist tendencies. Even though Cacabelos and its four thousand residents are located in the province of Castilla y León, it and they are close enough to the border with neighboring Galicia that *gallego* is the predominant language.

The walk took us through the El Bierzo valley. With the exception of a few farm paths through vineyards we strolled along pavement through a succession of small suburbs that extend from Ponferrada westward. The day's walk was only fifteen miles, but we were tired by the time we arrived in Villafranca Del Bierzo around 12:30.

Between Ponferrada and Villafranca del Bierzo

My walk that day was dedicated to the gratitude I felt for my friendship with Fr. Steve Dudek. We have known each other a long time, and are good friends. People will have relatively few really true good friends during their lifetime. Steve is one of mine, and I am fortunate. I hope I contribute some joy to his life in exchange for all he brings to mine. Fr. Steve is responsible for my first awareness of the Camino, as he and another friend—Fr. Mike Kuchar—were pilgrims on The Way in 2006.

Just before we rounded the bend to Villafranca Del Bierzo a farmer selling figs tried to sell us a bag for one euro. We tried one, thought it tasted good—very sweet—but did not want to lug a bag of figs around with us. We settled for four, two of which I ate while we walked. They gave me a bit of a queasy belly, but it did not last. Still, I was done with figs for awhile. Picaud's twelfth-century *Guide du Pèlerin* claimed—with an astonishing xenophobia for one so committed to promoting pilgrimage to St. James—"All fish and flesh—beef and pork—throughout Spain and Galicia makes foreigners ill."[9]

9. Kendall, *Medieval Pilgrims*, 55.

I wonder if figs should be on his list. The anonymous English fifteenth-century author of *Informacyon for Pylgrymes* would no doubt agree that they should:

> *And whan you come to dyvers havens beware of fruytes that ye ete none for nothynge; as melons and such colde fruytes; for they be not according to our complexion, and they gendre a bloody fluxe. And yf ony englyssheman catche there that sekeness, it is a great mervayle, but and he dye therof.*[10]

Too many figs gave this pilgrim a tummy ache
(Dmitri Popov, CC BY-SA 3.0, via Wikimedia Commons)

My guidebook led us through narrow, winding streets to Albergue Leo, a nicely restored three-story house operated by Maria—the granddaughter of the original owner. It was quite charming, with exposed beams, a central garden, a nice bar—restaurant, and a modern kitchen. Though it sounds basic, the fact that we were supplied with freshly laundered sheets and pillowcases to go with the luxurious, rustic blankets was an uncommon pleasure for an *albergue*.

We decided that we would take advantage of the kitchen to prepare our own meals, so we found a grocery store and bought what we needed for a delicious lunch of salami and cheese sandwiches topped with fresh tomato, lettuce, and balsamic vinaigrette. We also made salads with the same ingredients minus the bread. For dinner we would make spaghetti with meat sauce, more salad, and more bread. We topped it all off with some chocolate Twinkie—like things we saw on the grocery shelf that we could not resist.

10. Southern, *Retrospective*, 326.

If God continued to smile on our pilgrimage we'd walk into Santiago de Compostela one week from where we laid our heads in Villafranca Del Bierzo. I could hardly believe it. We had begun to think a bit about how we'd use our time between arriving there and leaving for home. Our primary goal was to complete the pilgrimage to Santiago de Compostela. If possible, we hoped to see Finisterre ("the end of the world")[11] and Muxia. We thought we might take in Santiago for a couple of days, then bus to Finisterre, spend the night, walk to Muxia, then bus back to Santiago for the flight home. We would try to nail down our plans in the next couple of days.

The next day we would be back into the mountains as we passed out of Castilla y León province and into the Camino's final and most westward state—Galicia. The climb would be very steep, and top out at the village of O Cebreiro, but we planned to stop about halfway up the mountain and stay at La Faba. This would allow us to tackle this difficult section in two days instead of one. With age comes some amount of wisdom!

Back into the mountains

11. Cartwright reminds us that before Columbus, the ocean to the west of Spain was "as outer space, and Spain, bordering on the ocean, was the end of the earth." The gospel—carried by St. James to Spain, and perhaps even by St. Paul—could be carried no further. Cartwright, *Catholic Shrines*, 13. To be fair, it seems that Westerners were a bit late to the game in recognizing the earth was not flat. Ibn Khurraddadhhih, postmaster of the Abbasid caliphate (820–912), described the earth as "a sphere . . . like the yolk in the interior of an egg." Romano, *Medieval Travel*, 112.

I looked forward to a phone call home later that day. It had been almost a week since I had spoken with Carol and I missed her very much. Very much.

Thanks for this stamp, Albergue Leo. You were a nice place to rest.

Up Some More. Seriously Up.

It was a chilly night in Villafranca Del Bierzo. This made for good sleeping under heavy blankets. We crept out of the bunk room and downstairs to the vacant bar area of the *albergue* to prepare our packs, tie shoes, collect our hiking poles, and get ready for the day.

It was dark, clear, breezy, and cold as we walked over the old Roman bridge, out of Villafranca Del Bierzo, and up into the mountains. Our headlamps reflected off our misty breaths. Though we could not see the mountains, we knew they were there because the brilliant dome of stars ended abruptly as we lifted our gaze upward. It was as if we were in a large bowl looking up toward the constellations. Beautiful.

Walking out of Villafranca Del Bierzo was like stepping into a starfield (Amanda Mocci amandamocci, CC0, via Wikimedia Commons)

The guidebook offered an alternative route for the first eleven kilometers of the walk to La Faba. We opted for the primary route since the alternative would have taken us steeply up into the mountains only to drop us down to the main path so we could re-climb the mountain for the final push toward O Cebreiro. And because the alternative path began in Villafranca, we would have been walking it in the dark, with the beautiful mountain views existing only in our imaginations.

When the skies eventually lightened we were high above the El Bierzo valley and strolling through mountain villages, grazing cows, chestnut forests, and fields of sheep—all muted by a wispy fog that later burned off to reveal the clear blue skies we'd grown accustomed to in Spain. This was one of the most beautiful places we had seen so far.

Now that we were back in forested country we could see evidence of logging operations from time to time. Logging trucks sometimes rumbled past us, and we saw stacks of cut trees waiting to be milled into lumber as we walked through some of the small towns like Pareje and Trabadelo.

The grade was gently but persistently upward since leaving the *albergue* and crossing over the river on our way out of Villafranca Del Bierzo. When we reached Herrerías,[12] the earth seemed to tilt. The last four kilometers to La Faba was straight up—like a ladder leaning against a house. This vertical section would continue the next day, taking us to the highest town on the Camino—Galicia's O Cebreiro.

Cairns in the stream near Herrerias

12. A town meaning "The Blacksmiths" and named for its long history of iron mining.

Sometimes when the walk grew boring or physically challenging, the way to take our minds off our legs and lungs was to write poetry. Or song lyrics. Here is the song we composed as I tried not to die on the climb to La Faba, sung to the tune of Allen Sherman's *Hello Muddah, Hello Faddah*:

Hello Muddah, Hello Faddah
Just walked outa' Ponferrada
This hill's a killah
Makes my lungs hollah
Hope my heart don't explode before La Faba

Loving Bruddah, Dearest Sistah
This mountain trail, gave me a blistah
It's fullah horse crap
It's rocky, mistah
At Disneyland it would be The Ankle Twistah

Mi amigo, mi compañero
Let's have no nightmares about tomorrow
We'll climb this mountain
And this I do know
We'll watch the sun come up in O Cebreiro!

Santiago Peregrino in the La Faba *albergue's* front yard

The La Faba *albergue* was run by a German association, with Roland and Ilona serving as our *hospitaleros*. The *albergue* was on the site of a former rectory for the adjacent church—the twelfth-century *Iglesia de San Andrés*. Both were destroyed in an earthquake some time ago. It had all been rebuilt, and was now very nice—simple, but nice. La Faba itself had little to offer except for a tavern, shop, and stunning *Sound of Music* views. The crowd at the *refugio* seemed like a nice bunch. It was chilly there. Long pants and fleece were part of the dress code once the warmth from the climb up the mountain wore off.

A fellow pilgrim drowses in the mountain sunshine at the La Faba *albergue*

La Faban prayers were offered in gratitude for the friendship of Kirk and Stephanie Brumels. What a wonderful couple. Before going to bed I prayed in the chapel for all of the intentions of this pilgrimage. I had the place to myself. It was a wonderful way to end a wonderful day.

Our La Faba *sello*

Into Galicia

We gave ourselves an extra thirty minutes to sleep so we would have some light on the stony mountain path as we hiked to O Cebreiro. I was awake by 5:30 anyway. Darnit.

We were a mix of Germans, Aussies, Americans, Spaniards, and Basques—who don't think of themselves as Spaniards—as we rustled our bags, drank coffee in the *albergue* kitchen, and laced up our shoes for the sixteen-mile hike over the mountain.

We met and enjoyed several conversations with Dan, an endodontist from Florida. He was going to finish the Camino about the same time as us, then bus back to Sarria (one hundred kilometers), meet his wife, who was flying over, and walk the last week again with her.

The walk up to O Cebreiro was a warm bit of work, but the air was cold and the stars brilliant as we climbed toward a slowly brightening sky. The sunrise behind us illuminated the cascading mountain ranges which seemed to stretch to eternity.

Just before reaching O Cebreiro we crossed over the border of Castilla y León and into our last region—Galicia. Different regions of Spain were, well, different. Galicia was green, wet, hilly, and filled with small farms. *Gallego* was the principal language, and was spoken by nearly 2.4 million people. My Spanish was adequate to pick out the occasional written word, but once one of the locals began speaking, I wanted to turn on the subtitles. *Gallego* has a lot in common with Portuguese, evidently, but it was, I am afraid to say, mostly Greek to me.

O Cebreiro was a very interesting village. Several of the buildings have thatched roofs in the Celtic style. The village was the home of Father Elías Valiña Sampedro, a local priest who was instrumental in the twentieth-century revival of the Camino de Santiago. He is said to have come up with the yellow arrow symbol and is also responsible for the *mojóns* in Galicia. He is buried in the handsome village church, and memorialized in the church's garden.

The thatched *palloza* of the highest village on the Camino—O Cebreiro
(gl:Usuario:Pablofc4, CC BY—SA 2.5 ES via Wikimedia Commons)

Most of the pilgrims we had seen since we began the Camino carried a scallop shell emblematic of the Camino de Santiago attached to their packs. Indeed, the scallop shell is such a powerfully ubiquitous symbol of pilgrimage that the shells have been found in the graves of long deceased pilgrims, presumably as a kind of good luck charm to hurry them successfully to the afterlife.[13] I was hesitant to add the shell to my ensemble until I felt like an authentic pilgrim. My arrival in O Cebreiro was when that happened. I purchased two shells, gave one to Joe as a gift, and fastened mine to my pack. It was official. I was a pilgrim.

Pilgrims to Santiago de Compostela can be known by their scallop shell
(José Antonio Gil Martínez from Vigo, Spain, CC BY 2.0 via Wikimedia Commons)

13. Webb, *Medieval European Pilgrimage*, 165. Webb reports that Denmark has more of these "scallop shelled" graves than any other medieval pilgrimage source.

The scallop shell has become a universal symbol of pilgrimage. Even the artist who carved the amazing eleventh-century bas-relief of Jesus, Cleopas, and the unnamed disciple on the road to Emmaus in the cloister of the abbey of *Santo Domingo de Silos* linked this biblical event to the *Compostelan* pilgrimage tradition. Nine centuries before the remains of St. James would be discovered in far northwest Spain Jesus is depicted with the traditional pilgrim's scrip (traveling satchel) adorned with the scallop shell.

Jesus with scrip and scallop shell as a pilgrim on the road to Emmaus in the abbey cloister at *Santo Domingo de Silos* (GFreihalter, CC BY-SA 3.0 via Wikimedia Commons)

We had enjoyed many, many beautiful days on the Camino, but that was the most beautiful yet. Stunning mountain vistas, beautiful deep valleys cloaked in shadow, and too many cow-filled pastures to count, each charming us with the tinkle of cowbells as the great brown beasts grazed away while ignoring us utterly. I hummed tunes from *The Sound of Music* in honor of the pastoral beauty of the area.

When the cathedral in Santiago de Compostela was being constructed, pilgrims carried a stone from the quarry near Triacastela to Santiago to do their bit in assisting the builders. While my backpack is light by any objective standard, toward the end of the day it can begin to feel like a burden. I honestly cannot begin to imagine carrying a one-hundred-pound stone from this place all the way to Santiago. To be perfectly frank, I doubt I could do it. And still, medieval folk walking barefoot—or perhaps shod in simple sandals or very thin boots—did this as a matter of routine.

We walked much of the day with our friends Sue and Brock. Both were lovely people with whom I hoped to stay in touch. We seem to have much in common and enjoyed each other's company.

I hoped the sense of spiritual discernment that was growing within me on the Camino (when I had hours to devote to prayer) would continue when I came home. I offered prayers for Tim Schoonveld on my first day in Galicia. He was a natural encourager, and had been so supportive of me, especially in the months preceding my pilgrimage. God bless him.

Joe and I had only five days before we walked into cathedral square at Santiago de Compostela. Only eighty-three miles left. The sense of accomplishment (and gratitude) for the ground that had been covered was somewhat balanced by two competing desires. One the one hand, we were anxious to arrive and complete our pilgrimage. On the other hand, we were enjoying the experience and feeling some degree of regret that its conclusion was imminent.

The last few miles leading to Triacastela were steeply, dangerously, toe-scrunchingly downhill. My feet and knees were glad to arrive at Albergue Berce do Camiño. I was ready to be done walking by the time that day was done. I spent so much time looking down that afternoon that I noticed that my shoes were starting to fall apart. The uppers had some splits that I hoped would not worsen before the week was out. The Hokas I purchased for that pilgrimage had performed admirably. They deserved a funeral with full honors when I got home.

We expected at least some rain over the next few days. I could not complain. The weather was perfect up until then. It did not owe us anything. Galicia is normally a very rainy place. It is green, verdant, and laced with streams and rivers. All of the water needed to create such a landscape was bound to fall on us eventually.

Pilgrim statue at *Alto de San Roque* endures the Galician winter
(Marathoni62, CC BY-SA 3.0 via Wikimedia Commons)

The next day we would walk through Sarria, which is where many, many pilgrims begin their Camino. It is the closest town from which one can walk to Santiago de Compostela and still earn the *compostela* from the cathedral. We expected the *albergues,* bars, and cafes to be much busier from that point forward. While I did not look forward to the increased Camino traffic, I vowed to do my best to adopt a spirit of welcome for each pilgrim. For each of us, Ian MacLaren reminds us, is fighting a great battle. I ought to do everything in my power to be helpful to those I meet along The Way.

When Carol and I visited Florence in 2015 we had the opportunity to see bedazzling Renaissance painting. While I marveled at the skills of artists such as Michelangelo, Donatello, Giotto, and others to capture their subjects in such a lifelike manner, I always wondered why they portrayed the feet of saints, martyrs, and other historic figures in such poorly rendered, outsized, even grotesque ways. After walking such a long way in shoes that were beginning to disintegrate and seeing how my own feet were evolving from their former state, I began to understand that the masters likely got it just right. I am guessing that people in ancient times walked a long way with inadequate footwear. They probably actually had grotesque-looking feet. Good job, Michelangelo.

**Carlo Crivelli and his bunioned, splay-footed Saint James Major, 1472
(Carlo Crivelli, Public domain, via Wikimedia Commons)**

As I crawled into bed I found myself grateful for the roof over my head and the mattress under my body. I was—and am—a very lucky person.

The stamp of Albergue Berce do Camiño

The Pilgrim Horde

Albergue Berce do Camiño was unusually, eerily quiet, with only eight pilgrims in residence. Joe and I had a room for four to ourselves. Unfortunately, my bed squeaked like it belonged in a Frankenstein movie. Every time I moved a muscle it creaked loud enough to wake the dead.

As we munched on Napoleons while walking out of town in the dark, the stars were bright, until Galicia's foggy mist enveloped us in an impenetrable fog. When it finally lightened up it was a misty day, with predictions of rain for later in the afternoon.

The stroll from Triacastela was through several farming villages with crowing roosters, mooing cows, and barking dogs. The paths were sunken between stone fences that appear to have been constructed by Divine order during Genesis's first six days. Great, hoary chestnut trees with massive, twisted trunks were our companions along the path. The chestnut (*Castanea sativa*) has existed in Spain since being introduced by the Romans. The fruit was a staple of the Galician diet until the eighteenth century, when a disease almost wiped them out. They are pressured again, as chestnut blight is taking a significant toll on the population, and may wipe the species out in Spain and France by 2040. A program of inoculating the trees with a nonlethal fungus was being attempted as a countermeasure.[14] I hoped the effort succeeds, because these massive trees added terrific character to that green land. They were the closest thing I'd yet seen to the anthropomorphic Ents of Tolkien's rapturously creative imagination or the grumpy apple trees in L. Frank Baum's haunted forest on the way to Oz.

If these trees could talk, what tales would they tell?

14. Nick Lloyd, "Chestnuts in Spain," http://www.iberianature.com/material/spain-chestnuts.html.

The trail rose and fell frequently, making for warm walking on an otherwise chilly morning. Though we could not see too far because of the mist, the landscape reminded me of New England.

After a few hours we walked into Sarria, which was a town of about twelve thousand people. It was positively chockablock with *albergues*, restaurants, cafes, and other hospitality services for pilgrims. Our stroll through the town took perhaps thirty minutes. Just before exhausting its many charms we walked past the *Monasterio de Magdalena* that hosted both an *albergue* and a primary school. It was midday, and the kids were outside in the schoolyard eating lunch and playing. It was a scene of everyday life that conjured thoughts of home. Soon. I would be home soon.

The scallop shell—the universal symbol of pilgrimage—decorating the bridge over the Rio Sarria in the town of the same name

We beat the rain into Barbadelo, a small village with a few *albergues* just a couple of kilometers beyond Sarria. This flyspeck of a village rated a mention in the *Codex Calixtinus* as an example of the commercial exploitation of the Camino. There isn't much commerce left to exploit nowadays.

A few years before our pilgrimage, the Galician *Xunta* undertook a program of replacing the *mojons* in the region. Unfortunately, it did not take long for the Camino philosopher-graffitists to have their way with these, as most were lavishly bestrewn with their musings and related artwork. And it was a sad fact that most of the brass mileage markers inset into the concrete structures had been pried out and now likely adorn pilgrim trophy shelves the world over. But those that remained reflected an uncharacteristic Galician mania for informing pilgrims of the exact distance from any given marker to the front steps of the Cathedral of Santiago de Compostela. And when I say *exact*, I mean accurate to three decimal places. Why in the world it matters to anyone if they were seventy-two kilometers from the cathedral instead of the 72.683 kilometers the mileage marker reported is, to put it charitably, a curiosity.

68.7746063 miles to go from Barbadelo. Exactly.

It was early when we arrived, and after only fourteen miles we could have gone farther, but we did not want to tempt fate or the rain so we pulled in at the first *albergue* we came to and declared it a good day. The hostel was modern and clean. We shared a bunk room with Syvia from Cologne, Dan from Florida, and Sven from Minnesota—all of whom we'd met previously and shared accommodation in earlier towns. Brock and Sue arrived about an hour after us and also decided to stay there. We were lucky to be able to stay in such a nice place for such a reasonable price. We had stayed in several municipal *albergues* on our pilgrimage. Some were OK. Others were, well, a place to sleep. The municipal *albergues* in Galicia are owned and operated by the state—the *Xunta de Galicia. Xunta albergues* are reputed to be Spartan experiences, often lacking doors on the bathrooms or curtains in the showers. While one adopts a certain casual attitude toward personal modesty while traveling in some parts of Europe, I preferred to shower without exposing my *peregrina* fellow travelers to my lathered, befoamed form. Call me old fashioned.

I rinsed out my shirt and underwear and hung them on the line, keeping a close eye on the skies. Fortunately, I was able to retrieve them about an hour later just as the skies opened.

I prayed for Cal and Eva Folkert as I walked that day. I was and am very grateful for their friendship. I also offered prayers of thanks for my family, whose patience and forbearance with me were allowing me to make the pilgrimage. I am lucky beyond measure. I received an encouraging email from Bob Moss when I logged into the *albergue's* Wi-Fi. What a terrific guy. He and his prostate cancer had been an object of my prayers during this pilgrimage. He was doing well, and I hoped he would continue to recover. Lindsey sent me some photos of Greta making funny faces—her specialty—and they really warmed my heart.

Joe and I tried to attend Mass in the twelfth-century *Iglesia de Santiago*. We walked about a kilometer through the countryside where we met an old man walking with a cane who was just about to open the church for what we thought would be a 6:00 Mass. We asked what time the Mass was and he responded in a mixture of Spanish, Gallego, and eldermumble. We thought we heard him say *seis y media*, so we followed him in, had our *credencial* stamped, and prayed on our own for awhile. Six-thirty came and went. No priest. No people. Just us and the old man. Hoping that some spiritual benefit might accrue to us for our good intentions, we walked back through the rain and went to dinner.

We tried to go to Mass in Barbadelo, but Barbadelo has no Mass *no mas*
(Gerd Eichmann, CC BY-SA 4.0 via Wikimedia Commons)

We were sixty-eight miles from Santiago de Compostela! My desire to reach the cathedral was like a mighty chain pulling me along The Way. I would do my best to discipline my mind to be able to enjoy and appreciate the people, sights, sounds, insights, and experiences that comprised the journey between Barbadelo and the relics of St. James.

The *sellos* of *Casa Barbadelo* and the *Iglesia de Santiago*
(complete with Santiago Matamoros theme)

Green Acres

It rained in the night, but we saw stars as we headed out of the *albergue*. As the sky brightened we saw cloudy skies with misty fields, but no rain. We were crossing our fingers that our luck would hold.

As we walked in the foggy darkness of a Galician *corredoira*—a sunken path between two ancient stone walls overhung by a canopy of tree boughs—we were blasted into near-incontinence by the braying of an invisible donkey not ten feet from us on the other side of one of the walls. It was like a sound track from a black-and-white horror movie. We had a good chuckle over it after recovering our composure.

We didn't see him, but we sure did hear him! (Florent Pécassou, CC BY-SA 3.0 via
Wikimedia Commons)

Our entire journey had been through agricultural areas, with the exception of the few big cities. The walk between Barbadelo and Ventas took this to new heights. We walked from barnyard to barnyard. By the end of the day we no longer noticed the smell of cow crap that so permeated the atmosphere. Speaking of cow crap, I just about wiped out after stepping in some in the inky dark. It was a close call. A couple of times we had to step aside and let herds of cows and sheep pass by. And for a few hundred yards I was treated to a stroll behind the east end of a line of westbound cows who filled the entire lane. Cows are gassy creatures, take it from me. Cows, sheep, and other ruminants are a major source of the world's methane emissions and add significantly to the problem of greenhouse gases. While one might be forgiven for thinking that most of this methane comes from bovine farts, in fact it comes mostly from bovine burps. I'm sure you've been dying to know this. Bring this up at your next party when the conversation begins to lag.[15]

The east end of westbound Galician cows

Galicia looks like Ireland or Scotland with rolling green hills and pastures of grazing sheep contained by ancient stone walls. It was beautiful, and one was given to whistling, humming, and the occasional song lifted to the verdant hills. Honestly, if a leprechaun jumped out from behind a hedge and tried talking me into following him to a pot of gold at the end of the rainbow, I do not think I'd have batted an eye in surprise.

The biggest news of the day is that we'd passed the one-hundred-kilometer post. We figured we were about fifty miles from Santiago de Compostela as I jotted notes in our *albergue* in Ventas de Narón, which we reached after twenty miles and nine long hours.

I prayed for Tonia Gruppen, Meg Frens, and Tim Koberna. I was proud to have them as Hope College's athletic trainers, and was grateful for

15. *Guardian*, "Methane Emissions."

their friendship. They did important, challenging work with Hope students, and they did it well.

We met several interesting people on the Camino that day. Sally from Phoenix was seventy years old, had done long hikes in twenty countries, and was carrying her son's ashes to spread at Finisterre. I couldn't get a word in edgewise, but she was an interesting person with whom to walk as we passed the one-hundred-kilometer marker.

A typical Galician *horreo*—a grain storage structure designed to keep vermin out of the seed. It seems hard to believe that a reasonably motivated mouse couldn't figure out how to outwit this system.

We stopped for a refreshing beverage in Morgade and got our *credencial* stamped. Afterward I walked ahead of Joe for about ninety minutes. It was not unusual for us to spend some time every day walking separately, but this was longer than normal. My gait is a bit longer and faster than his, but it's also true that Joe collected more souls when he walked than I did. Soul collecting is slow, patient work. Anyway, I waited for him after crossing the long bridge into Portomarín. At the end of the bridge there was a steep staircase that led up into the city. I was concerned that if I climbed the stairs and entered the city we might get separated. My stomach was beginning to send subtle signals suggesting the various benefits of a midday meal. My pack was bereft of any victuals, so I did not want to go poking around in a shop or cafe and have Joe walk past me unwittingly. Patience being a virtue, I sat down on the steps and waited. The Miño River was lovely to gaze upon. The green hills through which I had just passed occasioned peaceful thoughts. Twenty minutes passed. Where was Joe? Pilgrims passed by and we exchanged heartfelt *buen Caminos* with each other. One asked if I was in any distress. "Thank you, no. Just waiting for a friend." The fluffy white clouds formed various shapes and then broke apart to rearrange themselves anew. Twenty more minutes passed. Where are you, Joe? In fact, *where in the hell are you*? I resolved to give it ten more minutes and then I would don my pack and retrace my steps. Was he attacked by Galician cattle foaming with mad cow disease? Did he miss a yellow arrow or a scallop shell? Did he have a sudden, debilitating attack of gout? Was he writhing in a ditch with a painful, gouty foot? Did one of the more sinister-looking chestnut trees spout legs and inflict some terrible Entish punishment on him? *Should I run back to find him?!* Just as my patience morphed into concern and then degraded in an irrational blink to abject worry—in the ninth minute of my final ten-minute grace period—Joe popped out of the woods on the river's distant shore.

He ambled across the bridge nonchalantly, like a man without cares or concerns. "Hi there," I greeted him. "By any chance have you seen my friend Joe laying dead—or perhaps just gruesomely injured—anytime in the past ninety minutes or so? No? Oh, that's good. I'm sure he'll be along anytime now."

Joe explained that he met a woman—Jan from Korea—whose soul needed a bit of first-aid. Joe greeted her in his usual manner and she poured out her life story to him. She grew so emotional in conveying her sentiments for the pilgrimage that she broke down and wept. Once her waterworks were suitably primed, the broken relationships in her family were detailed and laid under the care of Joe's patient gaze. And this was her first day on the Camino. Joe did what he does best—he listened and was simply present to her during a time of need. What a guy. He was worth waiting for. Lunch could wait.

We hiked the last couple of kilometers from Hospital Alta da Cruz to Ventas de Narón with Stella—a recent college graduate from Rome. She was hoping to spend a year working with an NGO in Tunisia as part of an EU-funded program. She was a delightful conversationalist.

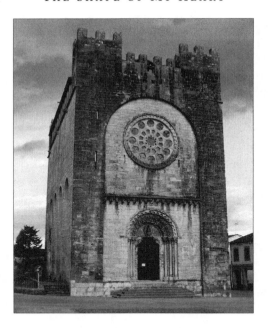

Portomarín's twelfth-century *San Xoán de Portomarín,* which was moved
—stone by stone—to its present location in the 1960s
(HombreDHojalata, CC BY-SA 3.0, via Wikimedia Commons)

After twenty tiring miles—the last six of which were unrelentingly uphill—we pulled into the *Casa Molar albergue* for the night. We were grateful that they still had two beds left, as this was the latest we'd walked thus far, not arriving until about 4:00.

We did not get too wet that day, which seems surprising given the gloomy forecast. I was not able to do laundry though, because it was pretty cloudy, cool, and spat just a bit of rain now and again. I would walk ripe to Melide the next day.

Stamps from Morgade and our Ventas *albergue—Casa Molar*

Damp, Green Galicia

It rained during the night—at times with some force. I was glad to be in the *albergue* and not on the road. The pavements were drying but we'd walk through fog thick enough to require my raincoat. The forecast called for a fifty-fifty chance of rain. Would our luck hold?

Albergue life at its best involves a happy spirit of shared struggles, even among strangers. It requires a spirit of self-denial and deference to the needs of others to work well. Casa Molar was a nice enough place, but I never caught the pilgrim vibe there. The woman in the bunk next to mine took both electrical outlets for her devices, leaving her equipment plugged in all night so nobody else could use them. She also experienced a nightmare which raised the hairs on the back of my neck when she shrieked in the night. The bunk room was full of bag rustlers who should know better by now. Well, only a few days to go.

The pilgrimage through the *meseta* section of the Camino was so different from the one we were experiencing in Galicia. There were similarities, of course, but while there were often long distances between towns out on the plains, green, damp Galician towns practically sprinkled the path. The towns were still tiny dots on the map, but there were just more of them.

We met a family of four from England. Mom, dad, and two children—ages eleven and nine—were walking together from St. Jean Pied-de-Port to Santiago de Compostela. Mom and Dad met twelve years before when they were pilgrims on the Camino. Now they were making the journey with their kids. They usually camped. Both kids wore matching straw hats and could not have been cuter. All were in good spirits. The nine-year-old boy—Fabian—was fascinated with my clip-on sunglasses. Where could one buy them? How much did they cost? Etc. I am glad someone besides me appreciated them.

Our walk that morning was very, very foggy. Even with headlamps we had a hard time seeing more than a few feet in front of ourselves. It did eventually rain, but not heavily and only intermittently. Our umbrellas came out, went up, and came down. Repeat, repeat, repeat.

Our guidebook informed us that there would be food available in many of the villages we passed through, but all were closed until we reached Palas de Rei at 10:30 about fifteen kilometers into our walk. We were starving, so we ordered a big breakfast of fried eggs, toast, bacon, and *cafe con leche*. It was delicious.

As we walked westward, we found ourselves meandering with increasing frequency through eucalyptus plantations. The trees freshened the air with a pleasant aroma that refreshed the air even as it calmed our spirits. Eucalyptus trees are native to Australia, and were imported to the Galician city of Pontevedra by the missionary monk Rosendo Salvado in 1863.[16] Eucalyptus grows quickly, and was originally used for fuel, charcoal, and in the construction of buildings—especially after the Spanish Civil War depleted the supply of native species—and native buildings. Eventually the eucalyptus was found to be an excellent source of pulp for papermaking—one of its principal uses by the time Joe and I walked through the verdant groves lining either side of The Way in Galicia.

Palas de Rei and its charming pilgrim rest stop
(Satna, CC BY-SA 4.0, via Wikimedia Commons)

Joe and I followed the most popular pilgrimage route to Santiago de Compostela—the *Camino Frances*. But there are many other ways for pilgrims to make their way to St. James. The earliest route—the *Camino Primitivo*—connects to the *Camino Frances* in Melide. King Alfonso II ("The Chaste") followed this route through the rugged northern interior in the ninth century when there were still lots of pesky Moors lurking about.

16. Ruiz and Lopez, "Review."

Melide was like so many small Spanish towns we had walked through. Many of these rural places lost significant population through external emigration to such places as Cuba, Switzerland, Argentina, and Germany. The good people of Melide also fit the pattern of looking for greater opportunity in Barcelona and Bilbao. The Camino economy was, for many towns, the principal part of their economy. Our guidebook calls most of the towns we walked through that day "nearly abandoned." We stopped in one of these—Ponte Campaña—to have our *credencials* stamped at Albergue Casa Domingo.

Peregrino Joe on The Way in green Galicia

We made a dinner of salad, pasta with chicken, and bread with our other bunk roommates. Carol and Saul were retired nurses from the Finger Lakes area of upstate New York who retired to Florida. It was fun to share food and stories of the Camino with each other.

Donna and Sam from Washington State were sharing our bunk room. They were a young couple hiking the *Camino Primitivo*. He had just finished solo hiking the Appalachian Trail. Impressive!

Eucalyptus trees—used in papermaking—were starting to line The Way

I received a most encouraging note from Tim Schoonveld. It was very nice, and I was grateful to receive it. Tim was a fine man whose email reminded me of the many, many people who were supporting me in my pilgrimage.

I offered prayers for Mark Husbands. He was a strong advocate for the kinds of things I tried to accomplish while provost at Hope. I was grateful for both his professional and personal support. I prayed that he would be successful in his burgeoning career as a college administrator.

We were thirty-two miles from the cathedral in Santiago de Compostela and the object of our pilgrimage. We had a twenty-mile walk to Arca followed by a twelve-mile walk to the cathedral on our last day. We talked about how we thought we would feel upon reaching the cathedral. I anticipated a sense of profound gratitude for the divine intervention that made it possible to walk all this way. But more importantly, I anticipated a sense of gratitude for the diminishing sense of anger and bitterness the pilgrimage has provided—through God's grace. I was looking forward to getting there. As I lay in my bunk I was reminded of how important it is to wean ourselves off the addictive self-harm that is anger:[17]

> *There is no sin nor wrong that gives a man such a foretaste of hell in this life as anger and impatience.* —Saint Catherine of Siena

17. Marshall, *Readings*, 335.

Sellos from *Casa Domingo* and *Albergue San Anton* in Melide

The Last *Albergue*

We awoke with the roosters—as usual. Because we had such a long walk to Arca we decided to have a breakfast of coffee and toast in the *albergue* before we left. It was terrifically foggy again. Our headlamps were not much help as they simply illuminated the suspended water droplets in the air, but we were completely blind without them in the dark.

We came across the British family camped near the path. They were cooking their breakfast. Because the nine-year-old boy—Fabian—had expressed so much interest in my flip-up sunglasses yesterday, I gave them to him as a gift. Now he would need to ask his parents if he could begin wearing eyeglasses so he'd have some use for my present!

I had a minor, somewhat embarrassing accident that morning. After we said goodbye to the Brits, I turned around and, without realizing where I was, I walked right into a creek. Fortunately, it was shallow and I only got wet feet—and a red face.

Tunnel of trees on the way to Arca

197

The weather gradually cleared, and by midday it was beautiful. Clear skies, mild breezes, and a fine temperature for walking. It clouded up and began to spit rain later in the day after dinner, but walking was very enjoyable on the way to Arca—once my wet feet dried.

On the way to Arca

Joe and I arrived at our *albergue* in Arca around 3:00. The Galician name for the town is O Pedrouzo. We were glad to be done walking after a twenty-one-mile day.

Staying in *albergues* had been an interesting and, perhaps, an important part of our pilgrimage. They were a good way to meet and spend time with other pilgrims. Most were fine, reasonably clean, with helpful *hospitaleros*. Still, by that point in the pilgrimage I was weary of bunk beds in dormitories. I wrote these lyrics to the tune of "Long Tall Mama Blues," by Jimmy Rodgers, while walking that day:

I been a-walkin' all over Spain
Ain't used a car, a bus, or a train
I've walked holes in both my hikin' shoes.

At night my head needs a place to lay
Somethin' better than a loft for hay
A place to rest after my dog-gone day

(Yodel) I got the albergue blues

The showers are cold and the rooms are dank
Eighty folks a-tootin' make a terrible stank
Albergues are a pit, take it to the bank.

(Yodel) I got the albergue blues

The toilet paper's gone, the bunk beds squeak
The kitchens are a mess, the pipes all leak
I could get more rest camped out in a creek.

(Yodel) I got the albergue blues

The bed bugs itch but only all night
The snorin' you hear will give you a fright
How can I sleep when they never turn off the light?

(Yodel) I got the albergue blues

When I get home I'll have a good night's sleep
In a nice quiet house with nary a peep
No crowing roosters roamin' 'round in the street.

(Yodel) I got the albergue blues

I shouldn't complain. We never had to sleep outside, and we were always treated with utmost hospitality. And not once did we have to find lodgings in a brothel, as the priest-pilgrim Felix Fabri had to on his first pilgrimage to the Holy Land.[18] No, not one of our lodgings was so interesting as that.

Gasoline for *peregrinos*

18. Kendall, *Medieval Pilgrims*, 66.

Many of the pilgrimage forums and guidebooks warn pilgrims to treat their clothing with permethrin as a preventative measure against bed bugs, which can sometimes be contracted in hostels along the way. Satan's Horses (as the Roma people call these pests)[19] produce a rash that causes terrific itching. Once contracted, the only effective treatment involves heating clothing, bedding, and backpack to a high enough temperature to kill both the insects and their eggs. This is a complaint well known to pilgrims down through the centuries. Swiss Dominican theologian and pilgrimage aficionado Felix Fabri recommended that Late Medieval pilgrims spend several hours each day picking these nuisances out of clothes and bedding lest they experience "unquiet slumbers."[20] Joe and I were grateful indeed to have avoided this plague, and thankful for the advice on applying permethrin to our gear, which we did before leaving for Spain.

My prayer intentions for the day's walk included Karen Pearson. I appreciated her friendship in so many ways. The fact that she took on the role of acting provost after my dismissal is something with which I was at peace. She was a fine person who I hoped would find joy and success in the role.

Joe and I would complete our pilgrimage the next day when we took a short twelve-mile walk into Santiago de Compostela. Our plan was to walk through the plaza in front of the cathedral to take in the sight and mark the moment, and then to head to the apartment we rented for a couple of days of rest and relaxation. We then planned to head back to the pilgrim office to receive our *compostela*, but probably would not be in time for the Saturday pilgrim Mass. We planned to go on Sunday instead. We also needed to figure out how, if, and when we would go to Finisterre and Muxia.

My emotions about the end of the pilgrimage were a jumbled mess on the eve of its final day. Gratitude, accomplishment, humility, and a hundred other feelings all combined in my head and heart. I just tried to stay open to how I might react when I finally knelt at the tomb of St. James.

We collected two stamps on the penultimate day of our pilgrimage—one at Bar Brea in Salceda and one at our very last *albergue*—La Porta de Santiago

19. Starkie, *Road to Santiago*, 244.
20. Kendall, *Medieval Pilgrims*, 71.

St. James. Finally

We woke at 6:30 after a good night's sleep anxious and eager to get on the road to Santiago de Compostela. It had rained during the night, but the pavement was drying and we could see a few stars. This was a hopeful and auspicious sign. We should have ignored it, for it rained most of the day—our first all-wet, all-day walk.

Around dawn we stumbled across the British family camped by the side of the path. Little Fabian was proudly sporting the flip-up sunglasses I gave him. He told us that they had walked until 1:00 am hoping to make it all the way to Santiago de Compostela, but had literally fallen asleep on the path during a rest break. Camping out another night after a thirty-five-kilometer day seemed the wisest choice to them under the circumstances.

Almost there

There were many pilgrims on the path as Santiago de Compostela drew closer. Many, many. I found myself pleased by this, and whispered a small prayer that they would all receive whatever it was that they needed.

I concluded my pilgrimage with prayers for my two former assistants—Lannette and Cristina. They were loyal friends and terrific helpers during my years as provost. The last six months had been hard for them. They deserved better, and I prayed their spirits would be renewed.

An encouraging pillar on the outskirts of Santiago de Compostela

Fifteen kilometers after leaving Arca we came to *Monte de Gozo* (Mount Joy).[21] A large sculpture honoring the Camino de Santiago is located there. In former times pilgrims would race each other to the top, with the winner proclaimed "king." That day I wore the regal crown as Joe arrived about ten minutes after me.

On a clear day the spires of the cathedral are said to be visible from this vantage point, but by the time Joe and I arrived the clear skies we had experienced at dawn were long gone. It was raining, and not gently. We could barely see the city. The cathedral spires? Forget about it. Samuel Purchas in his 1619 book, *Purchas His Pilgrimage*,[22] had this to say about Mount Joy:

> *Upon a hill stondez on hee*
> *Wher Sent Jamez ferst schalt thou see*
> *A Mount Joie mony stonez there ate*

Though Joe and I would walk alone from time to time, we committed to walking together from *Monte de Gozo* to the cathedral. The approach to the city was similar to other big cities through which we'd walked—just

---

21. Pilgrims to Jerusalem also get their first glimpse of the Old City from Palestine's Mount Joy. Bale, *Remembered Places*.

22. Quoted in Aviva, *Following*, 255.

wetter. We did not actually see the cathedral spires until we were just a few blocks away.

And suddenly—perhaps improbably—in the blink of an eye, we were there. Arrived. Finished. Eight hundred kilometers. Five hundred miles. 1,264,735 steps. The last yellow arrow. The last scallop shell. The last *mojón*.

Two drowned rats arrive at a cathedral under construction

The cathedral square was crowded with pilgrims and tourists, many visiting the market stalls set up in the square selling trinkets, crafts, and treats.[23] The cathedral's main facade was a disappointment, as it was largely covered in scaffolding while being repaired. Still, I think we would have spent some time simply soaking in the moment, but the skies opened with even more force than before. We were soon soaked despite our umbrellas and raincoats.

As disappointed as we were to see the cathedral wrapped in its scaffolding, the temple's *Praza de Obradoiro* was still a feast for the eyes—even in its rain-soaked dreariness. Among the most impressive structures that comprise the border of the plaza is the Parador Hotel. Constructed as a hospice to care for sick and injured pilgrims, the *Hospital de los Reyes Católicos* (Hospital of the Catholic Kings) was established by Ferdinand

23. Jonathan Sumption recounts the impression offered by German pilgrim Hieronymus Munzer, who said that Santiago de Compostela's citizens in 1494 were "fat as pigs and slothful at that, for they have no need to cultivate the soil when they can live off the pilgrims instead." Sumption, *Pilgrimage*, 288.

and Isabella in 1501 to mark the occasion of the capture of Granada from the Moors. Long before Generalissimo Ferdinand Franco ordered it transformed into one of Spain's premier luxury hotels, the hospital was described (in 1675) by Luis de Molina as "a crowning glory of Christendom."[24]

Hotel *Hostal de los Reyes Católicos* as seen from the porch of the cathedral
(Paradores, CC BY-SA 4.0, via Wikimedia Commons)

We made our way to the small shop about ten minutes' walk from the cathedral to pick up the keys to the efficiency apartment we rented for the next two nights. The proprietress—Mary—handed us the keys and we made our way a few doors down the street to the apartment. It was basic but met our needs perfectly.

After drying off and drying out we walked to a small restaurant near our apartment for hamburgers and Cokes. Even though we had a relatively light day of walking, twelve miles still helped us work up an appetite. Heck, we always had an appetite.

We were eager to receive our *compostela*,[25] which is the certificate attesting to our completion of the pilgrimage. We arrived at the pilgrim office to find a long line of *peregrinos* waiting patiently for their *compostelas*.

24. "Descripcion del Reino de Galicia," as quoted in Starkie, *Road to Santiago*, 45.

25. Medieval pilgrims frequently undertook the rigors of the road to Santiago de Compostela as part of an imposed penance for sins or as punishment for crimes. The modern *compostela* is the evolution of the letters these penitent-criminals brought home to prove they had finished the pilgrimage. Webb, *Medieval European Pilgrimage*, 51.

It took more than an hour for us to reach the front of the line. We were asked to hand over our *credencial* with its stamps of all the towns we had walked through on our way to Santiago de Compostela for inspection. Next, we were asked our nationality, age, and reason for our pilgrimage. Joe and I checked the box marked "religious." Finally, we were asked if we came by foot, horse, or bike. Once the woman running the show was satisfied that we were the real deal (I almost offered her a chance to examine my feet as evidence that we walked the entire way) we were given two artistically rendered certificates—one (in Latin) certifying that we'd made the pilgrimage and the other (mostly in Spanish) certifying our distance walked. We purchased protective tubes so the documents would not be damaged on the way home.

The Pilgrim Office made it official when they issued us our *compostela*

We were anxious to see the cathedral, but when we arrived they were shooing tourists from the building so a Mass could be conducted. Since we were planning to attend the noon Mass on Sunday—the following day—we decided to just head to the grocery store to obtain items for dinner and tomorrow's breakfast. Dinner was a heaping plate of chicken in mushroom gravy, onions, potatoes, tomato wedges, and ice cream for dessert. We made too much, and felt fine about it.

Had the main entrance to the cathedral not been closed for conservation, we would
have been able to marvel at the *Portico de Gloria*, which has been described as "the
most overwhelming monument of medieval sculpture."[26]
(Joaquim Morelló, Public domain, via Wikimedia Commons)

We were very tired, and looked forward to a good sleep with no alarm
clock to wake us. Also, no roosters cock-a-doodle-dooing, no pilgrims
rustling bags, coughing, farting, and generally making a racket.

We did not have very much to accomplish the next day other than the
pilgrim Mass at noon followed by a tour of the *Museo das Peregrinaciós
e de Santiago* (Museum of Pilgrimage). We wrote to Brock, Sue, Reinhard,
and Heide to see if they'd like to have dinner together if they'd be in town. It
would be fun to break bread with these new friends one more time.

We collected three stamps today—two from cafes along the way,
and the third from the cathedral's Pilgrim Office

26. Porter, *Romanesque*, 263.

Santiago de Compostela

I slept the sleep of the innocent during our first night in Santiago de Compostela, with a comfortable bed, a nice bedspread, no snoring, and the sure knowledge that our walking days were behind us. I fell asleep at 10:00 and slept without interruption until 8:00. *Awesome* is an overused expression these days, but that is just what it was.

St. James looked a bit surprised to see us (Luis Miguel Bugallo Sánchez [Lmbuga Commons][Lmbuga Galipedia], CC BY-SA 3.0, via Wikimedia Commons)

Our first priority for the day was to officially end our pilgrimage by attending the pilgrim Mass in the cathedral. We had been given a heads-up by another pilgrim that we should be ninety minutes early if we wanted a seat. This turned out to be excellent advice. We were in line at 10:30 for the noon Mass, and were lucky enough to get a seat in one of the first pews in the cathedral's transepts. From this vantage point we were able to see the celebrant (though not the children's choir, which was excellent) and the *botafumeiro* in action. This diesel-engine-sized censer weighs 175 pounds and is swung across the cathedral's transept dispensing clouds of incense as it hurdles at nearly fifty miles per hour above the head of the unwashed masses. Eight men—broad of shoulder and bulging of biceps—pull on the rope that gets the thing moving and urging it on to greater heights, until it nearly touches the ceiling. It would not hurt for long if it hit you.[27]

27. *Botafumeiro,* http://catedraldesantiago.es/liturgia/#botafumeiro.

Smelly pilgrims were evidently a real problem in medieval times when bathing habits and standards of personal cleanliness were much different than today. In 1474 a wealthy pilgrim to Aachen left money to have two baths built—one at each end of the town for the use of pilgrims as they transited the city.[28] I admit that it was cool to be able to see the *botafumeiro* swing high over our heads, almost touching the cathedral ceiling.

The *botafumeiro* being prepared to soar to the cathedral's heights
(Gerd Eichmann, CC BY-SA 4.0, via Wikimedia Commons)

The Mass was an emotional experience. I was mindful of celebrating the Eucharist with two thousand fellow pilgrims, some of whom likely took a bus to get to Santiago de Compostela and others who walked knee-shattering distances and endured great hardship to do so (like the man from the Netherlands next to us who walked from The Hague). I was mindful of the many holy men and women who had made the same journey I had, including St. Francis of Assisi. I was pleased to be able to take some time in that setting to give thanks for the spiritual blessings of the pilgrimage, including the degree to which my anger had abated. And the Mass was a good opportunity to pray for the courage required to take what I had learned over the previous five weeks and continue it, turning what life was left to me into a pilgrimage, always seeking greater, deeper communion with God.

28. Webb, *Medieval European Pilgrimage*, 112.

**Reliquary of St. James the Apostle in the crypt of the cathedral
of Santiago de Compostela**

After Mass we visited the *Museo das Peregrinacións e de Santiago*, dedicated to displaying the history, art, and culture of the pilgrimage phenomenon, and especially the Camino de Santiago. We were admitted without charge since it was Sunday. It was an excellent museum, and provided some good ideas for the senior seminar I hoped to teach once I resumed my professorial duties.

The city was jammed with people. Just loaded. Filled. Many (*most?*) were older tourists, some who appeared to be part of tour groups by virtue of their matching yellow hats or neckerchiefs. But there were also lots and lots of "traditional" pilgrims like us. Some we recognized from our travels and others were new faces. Some seemed to stroll the streets in seeming comfort and familiarity while others—likely who just arrived—seemed a bit overwhelmed, just as we had been when we had concluded our Camino the day before.

Pilgrims gather in the *Praza de Obradoiro*
(Reservas de Coches, CC BY 2.0, via Wikimedia Commons)

An anonymous medieval Venetian pilgrim described Burgos as "fine, large, and well-populated," León as "not very fine," and Santiago de Compostela as "small and dirty—piggish."[29] This Venetian was all wet. My early impressions of Santiago were positive indeed. Small? Certainly not. Dirty? No more so than any other big city, and far less than many. Piggish? I haven't the faintest idea what he meant by this, but on behalf of pilgrims everywhere, I apologize to the city for this egregious lack of manners.

We planned to rest in Santiago de Compostela for a couple of days, and then spend one day each in Finisterre and Muxia on the coast before returning to the city and flying home. My longing for home was a physical ache, and the rest of the time in Spain a kind of limbo to be endured. I would do my best to enjoy the sights of the city and the wonders of the Spanish coastline, but my heart was at home. As were my true loves.

29. Webb, *Medieval European Pilgrimage*, 180.

The Continuing

To the Coast of Death

J OE and I took the bus to Finisterre after leaving Santiago de Compostela. We spent one evening there. We hiked out to the lighthouse at "the end of the world." It was an impressive setting, but could be more wonderful if visitors would only pick up their trash. Litter bloomed like flowers in spring. The views were truly astounding, though, and the sight of such a vast expanse of open water—a rare experience for most people—reminded me of how beautiful Holland, Michigan, USA, with its Lake Michigan shoreline is. We're lucky.

Our pilgrimage didn't end at the tomb of St. James

While in Finisterre I received an email from Heide and Reinhard informing us that they were changing their plans so they could see us one more time. We agreed to meet in Muxia the next day. This was a very touching gesture.

The final *mojón* at Cape Finisterre was a welcome sight

We took another bus from Finisterre to Cee, and then transferred to a small bus—an extended van, really—for the ride to Muxia. The bus/van had balding tires and the driver must have had NASCAR aspirations. He drove like a bat out of hell around curves, down steep hills, through sleepy villages—you name it, he sped through it. I was grateful to get out of that vehicle on a gorgeous harborside street in Muxia.

It was lunchtime when we arrived in Muxia, so we went into the first cafe we saw and ordered sandwiches. Ten minutes later Heide and Reinhard showed up! We enjoyed a nice chat, catching up on all we had seen and done since parting ways on the Camino last week.

After lunch we walked about one kilometer to the church—*Nosa Señora de Barca*—at the end of the peninsula. It was fantastically beautiful—every bit the match of Finisterre. We spent quite a bit of time there taking photos and just soaking in the views and the fine weather.

Muxia and *Nosa Señora da Barca* (Our Lady of the Boat)

After checking into our lodging and cleaning up a bit we attended Mass with Heide, and then met Reinhard for dinner. Most of my meals in Spain have been of the pilgrim variety. In Finisterre and Muxia I vowed to try some of the local specialties. In Finisterre I enjoyed *zorza*—pork slices cooked in a mild green sauce and served on a bed of French fries. It was good, but there was so much of it that I could not eat it all. For our dinner with Heide and Reinhard in Muxia I had *pimientos* (a plate full of small green chilis cooked in olive oil and seasoned with coarse sea salt) and calamari. It was delicious.

Pilgrims at large in Muxia

We traded hugs with Heide and Reinhard after dinner, promising to keep in touch. Reinhard has walked the Camino five times, and would do so again the next summer in 2017, when he was seventy-three. Heide would go too. He wanted us to join him. I thanked him, but explained that I have a job to which I must return, and that my heart was not made to be away from Carol for so long.

Our final *sellos* from Finisterre and Muxia

As I sat in front of Muxia harbor recording these thoughts while waiting for the bus back to Santiago de Compostela and the airport, I could honestly say that the Camino was finished for me. I am so grateful for the experience and the insights it provided. As I prepared to leave Spain I could only hope that my pilgrimage through life would continue, and that the things I learned there would bear fruit back home. Neither finishing that pilgrimage nor experiencing the spiritual renewal it provided were inevitable. I was profoundly grateful.

The bus whisked us away from the Muxia harborside for our wild hairpinning ride back to the city. We spent our last night in Spain in a hotel in Lavacolla—a nearby suburb. As our final nod to the pilgrim journey, the alarm rang at 4:00 am. We rose, dressed according to the habit of the past six weeks, affixed headlamps, and walked to the airport.

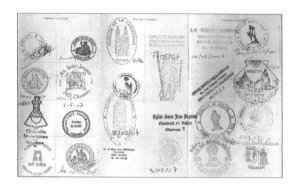

If pilgrimages are about the journey and not the destination, we were grateful for all of the places that comprised our journey (Scanned and uploaded by Jane023: June 2007, Public domain, via Wikimedia Commons)

Finally

O N April 18, 2018, I drove across the state to attend my Uncle Joe's funeral. I walked into Our Lady of Sorrows Church and found a place in the middle of the sanctuary. As I knelt to offer my prayers for the repose of my uncle's soul, my eyes lifted and took in the mural that filled the entire wall behind the tabernacle. In the three seconds it took me to scan the scene I was transported back to the Camino and to the dozens of churches Joe and I visited as we walked toward Santiago de Compostela. Suddenly I was in Spain again. There was Mary in the central focal spot. Jesus was there, but he seemed to be present as a commentary on Mary's dolefulness. And as in Spain, his image was so high on the wall that most in the church could not see him. To Mary's right was St. Peter with his crossed keys, binding and loosing on earth as in heaven. And to Mary's left was my old friend, *Santiago Peregrino*. His wide-brimmed hat was admittedly more Renaissance than medieval. And while his signature scallop shell was omitted by the muralist,[1] his staff and water gourd were not only present, but were being presented to him by an angel who pointed to some far and distant place, as if saying, "Go!"[2]

1. Jean Charlot, see https://www.jeancharlot.org/.
2. Shiffer, "Pencil Madonna."

Go![3]

The Camino, it seems, is in me and I in it. I cannot help seeing its influence in so many places, and often at unexpected times. I think of our pilgrimage every day. What's more, I remember with gratitude the healing, grace, and forgiveness I experienced while a pilgrim to St. James. Will it always be thus? I pray that it will be, for I hope to never forget or lose sight of God's goodness and his love for me. I am not in Compostela anymore, but Compostela—and so much more—is in me.

And the shape of my heart has changed for the better.

Richard Ray
Christmas 2021
Holland, Michigan

3. *Our Lady of Sorrows and Ascension of Our Lord* (full image with subsequent detail). Artist: Jean Charlot. July 10–August 16, 1961. Fresco. Approximately 1300 square feet. Ceiling and apsidal wall, Church of Our Lady of Sorrows, Farmington, Michigan. © The Jean Charlot Estate LLC. With permission.

Bibliography

Alighieri, Dante. *Divine Comedy, Longfellow's Translation, Complete*. S.I.: Pub One Info, n.d.

Anonymous. "The Pilgrims' Sea Voyage and Seasickness." poetrynook.com/poem/pilgrims-sea-voyage-and-seasickness.

Auden, W. H. "Atlantis." https://allpoetry.com/poem/8492995-Atlantis-by-W-H-Auden.

Augustine, Saint. "Office of Readings." http://www.liturgies.net/Liturgies/Catholic/loh/lent/week1sundayor.htm.

Aviva, Elyn. *Following the Milky Way: A Pilgrimage on the Camino de Santiago*. Santa Fe: Pilgrims' Process, 2001.

Ayuntamiento de Carrión de los Condes. "Himno-Carrión." http://www.carriondelos condes.org/wp-content/uploads/2014/06/Himno-Carrión.pdf.

Ayuntamiento de Tardajos. "Camino de Santiago Tardajos." https://www.tardajos.es/content/camino-de-santiago.

Bale, Anthony. "Mount Joy: The View from Palestine." *Remembered Places* (blog), January 21, 2014. https://rememberedplaces.wordpress.com/2014/01/21/mount-joy-the-view-from-palestine/.

Ball, Suzanne. "Camino de Santiago: A Stone & a Prayer at Cruz de Ferro." *TravelSmart Woman* (travel blog), January 1, 2017. https://travelsmartwoman.com/cruz-de-ferro/.

Barber, Malcolm. *The New Knighthood: A History of the Order of the Temple*. Cambridge: Cambridge University Press, 1994.

Beevor, Antony. *D-Day: The Battle for Normandy*. London: Viking, 2009.

Berry, Wendell. *Remembering: A Novel*. Berkeley, CA: Counterpoint, 2008.

Canoves, Gemma. "Rural Tourism in Spain: An Analysis of Recent Evolution." *Geoforum* 35 (2004) 755–69.

Carter, Michael. "Why We Can Have Faith in Relics of the True Cross, Whatever Their True Age." *Tablet*, March 29, 2021. https://www.thetablet.co.uk/blogs/1/1756/why-we-can-have-faith-in-relics-of-the-true-cross-whatever-their-true-age.

Cartwright, John K. *The Catholic Shrines of Europe*. New York: McGraw-Hill, 1955.

Cassian, John. *John Cassian: The Conferences*. No. 57. New York: Newman Press, 1997.

Cervantes-Godoy, Dalila. "The Role of Agriculture and Farm Household Diversification in the Rural Economy of Spain." OECD.org. http://www.oecd.org/agriculture/agricultural-policies/43245602.pdf.

Chaucer, Geoffrey. *The Canterbury Tales*. Verse translation, introduction, and notes by David Wright. Oxford: Oxford University Press, 1986.

Cross, Samuel Hazzard, and Olgerd Sherbowitz-Wetzor. *The Russian Primary Chronicle: Laurentian Text*. Cambridge, MA: Medieval Academy of America, 1953.

Dintaman, Anna, and David Landis. *Hiking the Camino De Santiago: Camino Frances; St. Jean—Santiago—Finisterre*. 3rd ed. Village to Village Guide. Harrisonburg, VA: Village to Village, 2016.

The English Version of the Book V (Codex Calixtinus). http://codexcalixtinus.es/the-english-version-of-the-book-v-codex-calixtinus/.

Evans, Percy Griffith. *A Critical Annotated Edition of El Passo Honroso De Suero De Quiñones by Pedro Rodríguez Delena*. Urbana, IL: n.p., 1930.

Fletcher, Richard. *The Quest for El Cid*. New York: Oxford University Press, 1989.

Ford, Richard, et al. *A Handbook for Travellers in Spain, and Readers at Home*. Centaur Classics. London, 1845.

Francomano, Emily C. "The Legend of the *Tributo de Las Cien Doncellas*: Women as Warweavers and the Coin of Salvation." *Revista Canadiense de Estudios Hispánicos* 32 (2007) 9–25.

Freeman, Charles. *Holy Bones, Holy Dust: How Relics Shaped the History of Medieval Europe*. London: Yale University Press, 2011.

Funk, Mary Margaret. *Thoughts Matter: The Practice of the Spiritual Life*. London: A&C Black, 1998.

Garver, Valerie L., and Owen M Phelan. *Rome and Religion in the Medieval World: Studies in Honor of Thomas F. X. Noble*. London: Taylor & Francis, 2016.

Gerritsen, Willem P., and Anthony G. van Melle, eds. *A Dictionary of Medieval Heroes: Characters in Medieval Narrative Traditions and Their Afterlife in Literature, Theatre, and the Visual Arts*. Translated by Tanis Guest. Woodbridge, UK: Boydell, 1998.

Guardian. "Methane Emissions from Cattle Are 11% Higher than Estimated." *Guardian*, September 29, 2017. https://www.theguardian.com/environment/2017/sep/29/methane-emissions-cattle-11-percent-higher-than-estimated.

Hammond, Peter. "Film Review: Luther." ReformationSA.org. http://www.reformationsa.org/index.php/component/content/article/61-film-reviews/167-film-review-luther.

Hinojosa Montalvo, José. *Los Judíos en la España Medieval: De la Tolerancia a la Expulsión*. Instituto de Estudios Almerienses, 2000. http://hdl.handle.net/10045/13209.

Hobbes, Thomas. *Leviathan*. Edited by John Charles Addison Gaskin. Oxford World's Classics. Oxford: Oxford University Press, 1998.

Kendall, Alan. *Medieval Pilgrims*. New York: Putnam, 1970.

Kosloski, Phillip. "Here's Why a Pilgrimage Is an Important Aspect of Spiritual Life." *Aleteia*, May 15, 2018. https://aleteia.org/2018/05/15/heres-why-a-pilgrimage-is-an-important-aspect-of-the-spiritual-life/.

Lee, Laurie. *As I Walked Out One Midsummer Morning*. Boston: Godine, 2011.

Marshall, Jonathan, ed. *Readings in Church History*. Hiram, ME: Hubbard Hill, 2009.

McNeill, John T., and Helena M Gamer. *Medieval Handbooks of Penance: A Translation of the Principal "Libri Poenitentiales" and Selections from Related Documents*. Records of Western Civilization. New York: Columbia University Press, 1990.

Merton, Thomas. *Thoughts in Solitude*. New York: Farrar, Straus and Giroux, 2011.

Metropolitan Museum of Art. *The Art of Medieval Spain: A.D. 500–1200*. New York: Abrams, 1993.

Michener, James A. *Iberia: Spanish Travels and Reflections*. Random House, 1968.

Moseley, Christopher, ed. *Atlas of the World's Languages in Danger*. 3rd ed. Paris: UNESCO, 2010. http://www.unesco.org/languages-atlas/.

Mullins, Edwin. *The Pilgrimage to Santiago*. Northampton, MA: Interlink, 2001.

O'Reilly, James, et al., eds. *The Best Travel Writing 2011: True Stories from around the World*. San Francisco: Travelers' Tales, 2011.

Porter, Arthur K. *The Romanesque Sculpture of the Pilgrimage Roads*. Boston: Marshall Jones, 1923.

Ragazzoli, Chloé, et al., eds. *Scribbling through History: Graffiti, Places and People from Antiquity to Modernity*. London: Bloomsbury, 2018.

Romano, John F. *Medieval Travel and Travelers: A Reader*. Toronto: University of Toronto Press, 2020.

Roxburghe Club, et al. *The Itineraries of William Wey . . . to Jerusalem, A.D. 1458 and A.D. 1462; and to Saint James of Compostella, A.D. 1456; from the Original Manuscript in the Bodleian Library*. London: Nichols, 1857.

Ruiz, Federico, and Gustavo Lopez. "Review of Cultivation, History and Uses of Eucalypts in Spain." Conference paper. September 2010. https://www.researchgate.net/publication/258112099_Review_of_cultivation_History_and_Uses_of_Eucalypts_in_Spain.

Shiffer, Kathy. "The Pencil Madonna: A Modern Rendition of Our Lady of Sorrows." *Patheos*, September 15, 2012. http://www.patheos.com/blogs/kathyschiffer/2012/09/the-pencil-madonna-a-modern-rendition-of-our-lady-of-sorrows/.

Socks, Pete. "Church Fathers, Day 287: St. Ephrem Says Control Your Anger before You Pray". *Patheos*. May 4, 2015. http://www.patheos.com/blogs/catholicbookblogger/2015/05/04/church-fathers-day-287-st-ephrem-says-control-your-anger-before-you-pray/.

Southern, Henry. *The Retrospective Review*. London: Baldwyn, 1820.

Starkie, Walter. *The Road to Santiago: Pilgrims of St. James*. London: Murray, 1957.

Sumption, Jonathan. *Pilgrimage*. London: Faber & Faber, 2011.

Telegraph reporters. "The Patron Saint of the Internet Is St. Isidore, Who Tried to Record Everything Ever Known." *Telegraph*, September 6, 2018. https://www.telegraph.co.uk/technology/0/st-isidore-patron-saint-internet.

Teller, Simon. "Preaching the Word, without Words." *Dominicana*, May 3, 2018. https://www.dominicanajournal.org/preaching-word-without-words/.

Trueman, Chris N. "Roman Roads." March 16, 2015. https://www.historylearningsite.co.uk/ancient-rome/roman-roads/.

United Nations Educational, Scientific and Cultural Organization. "Memory of the World." http://www.unesco.org/new/en/communication-and-information/memory-of-the-world/register/full-list-of-registered-heritage/registered-heritage-page-8/the-decreta-of-leon-of-1188-the-oldest-documentary-manifestation-of-the-european-parliamentary-system/.

"Valdeviejas Celebra la Fiesta del Ecce Homo." *Astorga Redacción*, May 3, 2018. https://astorgaredaccion.com/art/18380/valdeviejas-celebra-la-fiesta-del-ecce-homo.

Vázquez de Parga, Luis, et al. *Las Peregrinaciones a Santiago de Compostela, Etc. [by L. Vázquez de Parga, J. M. Lacarra and J. Uría Ríu. With a Bibliography, Maps and Plates.]*. 3 vols. Madrid, 1948.

Webb, Diana. *Medieval European Pilgrimage c. 700–c. 1500*. London: Palgrave, 2002.

Wilkinson, Isambard. "Spain's 'Damned' Maragatos Seek Salvation." *Telegraph*, August 16, 2003. https://www.telegraph.co.uk/news/worldnews/europe/spain/1439069/Spains-damned-maragatos-seek-salvation.html.

Wilson, Joseph. "Ex-Catalan Leader Vows to Keep Fighting Extradition to Spain." *APNews*, March 7, 2021. https://apnews.com/article/europe-carles-puigdemont-spain-belgium-europe-1ed11b0e0f199470733a15df84823c82.